FRANK THOMPSON

FRANK THOMPSON

HER CIVIL WAR STORY

by Bryna Stevens

MACMILLAN PUBLISHING COMPANY
New York

MAXWELL MACMILLAN CANADA
Toronto

MAXWELL MACMILLAN INTERNATIONAL
New York   Oxford   Singapore   Sydney

The publisher would like to thank Dr. Russell F. Weigley, Distinguished University Professor of Temple University, for his comments and suggestions.

Photographs on pages 20 and 124 from the collection of the Michigan State Archives, Department of State. All other illustrations from *Nurse and Spy*, 1865

Macmillan Publishing Company is part of the Maxwell Communication Group of Companies.

Macmillan Publishing Company
866 Third Avenue, New York, NY 10022

Maxwell Macmillan Canada, Inc.
1200 Eglinton Avenue East, Suite 200
Don Mills, Ontario M3C 3N1

First edition
Printed in the United States of America

10 9 8 7 6 5 4 3 2 1

The text of this book is set in 11 point Baskerville.
Book design by Constance Ftera.

Library of Congress Cataloging-in-Publication Data
Stevens, Bryna.
    Frank Thompson : her Civil War story / by Bryna
Stevens. — 1st ed.   *10423*
        p.   cm.
    Includes bibliographical references and index.
    Summary: A biography of the woman who, disguised as a man, moved behind Confederate lines to spy for the Union during the Civil War.
    ISBN 0-02-788185-7
    1. Edmonds, S. Emma E. (Sarah Emma Evelyn), 1841–1898—Juvenile literature.   2. United States—History—Civil War, 1861–1865—Secret service—Juvenile literature.   3. Spies—United States—Biography—Juvenile literature.   4. Impostors and imposture—United States—Biography—Juvenile literature.   [1. Edmonds, S. Emma E. (Sarah Emma Evelyn), 1841–1898.   2. Spies.   3. United States—History—Civil War, 1861–1865—Secret service.]   I. Title.
    E608.E235S74   1992   973.7'85'092—dc20   [B]   91-45382

Dedicated to the rebel in all of us.

Contents

Author's Note

Emma Edmonds Seelye lived about one hundred years ago, yet her life is still relevant. I found Emma's story appealing because it told me how one young woman struggled to find her way in a male-dominated society, as many women are doing now.

Growing up in a farm community in Canada at a time when women were completely dominated by men, Emma rebelled. Women today have some laws to protect their rights; in Emma's day such laws did not exist. Left to her own devices, Emma decided to solve her problems by running away from home and pretending to be a young man. Her disguise brought difficulties, but privileges as well. She enjoyed the freedom men did, freedom to pursue activities she'd never experienced before, such as serving as a soldier, nurse, and spy for the North during the Civil War.

In Emma's day, women could not serve in the armies of either North or South. So Emma's reactions and experiences will still be of interest to readers today, as women, in increasing numbers, are serving in our nation's armed forces.

Since disguising herself as a man was in itself a lie, Emma's truthfulness about the experiences related in her book, *Nurse and Spy*, has been questioned. She often uses wrong names and initials, perhaps to protect herself and the privacy of others. Readers, therefore, must decide for themselves how much to believe, though a great deal of her story *has* been documented by Union Army officers, congressmen, and others. I believe Emma's account to be mainly true, but I also think she exaggerated somewhat to make her life seem more exciting, just as others have been known to do in their own lives from time to time.

In researching Emma's story I used mainly her account in *Nurse and Spy*, first published in 1865. The original publisher's introduction to the book can be found in the Appendix. Another source was a 1960 biography by Sylvia Dannett titled *She Rode with the Generals*. For more information on Emma and the Civil War in general, you can refer to the Sources section at the end of this book.

I have used long quotations from Emma's book (spelling and punctuation have been modified somewhat to conform to modern style). Readers may find Emma's style of writing fanciful and elaborate by today's standards, yet her first-hand account gives us the flavor of life in Civil War days. Some of her descriptions will seem quite familiar, as when she compares fresh country air to the "choky stuff" of the cities, reminding us that pollution is not a new problem.

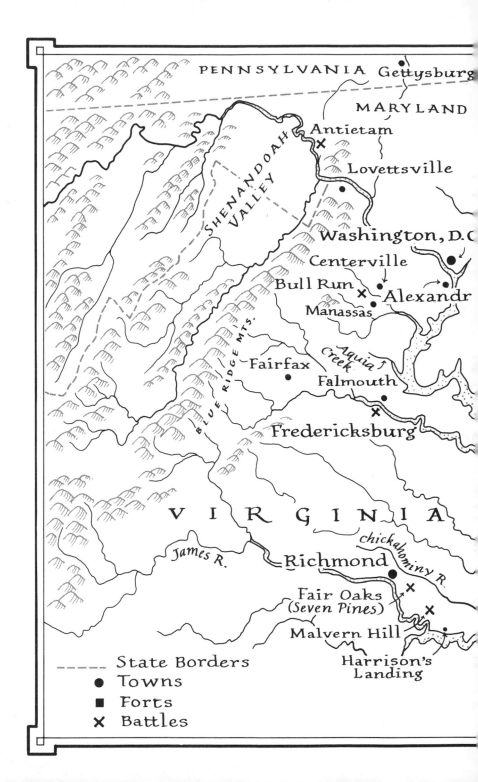

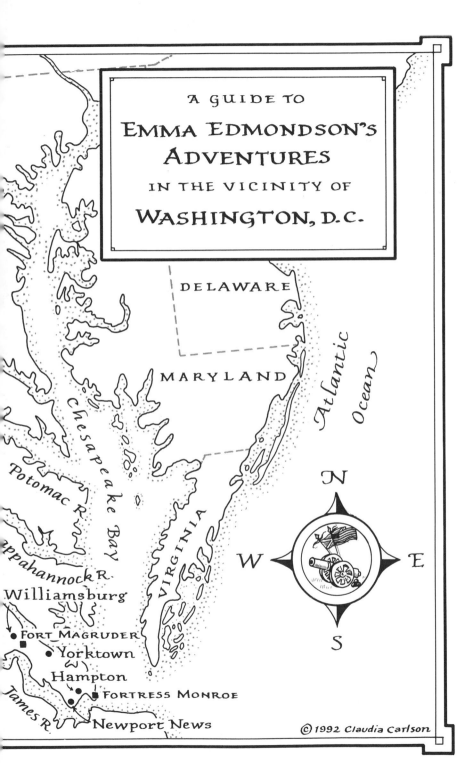

A GUIDE TO
EMMA EDMONDSON'S
ADVENTURES
IN THE VICINITY OF
WASHINGTON, D.C.

DELAWARE

MARYLAND

Atlantic Ocean

Chesapeake Bay

Potomac R.

VIRGINIA

ppahannock R.

Williamsburg

● Fort Magruder

● Yorktown

Hampton

■ Fortress Monroe

James R.

Newport News

N
W E
S

© 1992 Claudia Carlson

── 1 ──

Leaving Home

If it hadn't been for her father, Isaac Edmondson, fifteen-year-old Sarah Emma might not have run away. But Emma felt she had no choice. After all, why should she have to marry a man she didn't love and never could, a man much older than herself?

Emma wasn't actually certain she wanted to marry, at least not yet. She thought traveling and searching for adventure would be a lot more fun. She'd gotten the traveling idea years before, when she was only nine. A peddler who stopped at the family farm in Magaguadavic, in the province of New Brunswick, Canada, gave her a book, *Fanny Campbell, The Female Pirate Captain: A Tale of the Revolution!*, a story about a young girl who disguised herself as a man and went to sea to rescue her sweetheart from pirates. Emma was certain the story was true.

Perhaps the peddler had given the book to Emma because she seemed so lively, much livelier than any of her three older sisters. Emma's mother, Betsy, often worried about her adventurous Emma, who chose the wildest colt to ride, hunted with her father's shotgun, and climbed to the top of the tallest building she could find. Not surprisingly, Emma loved reading about Fanny, a noble-looking girl who could shoot a panther and ride the wildest horse and "do almost any brave and useful act." When Emma first read of Fanny's exploits, she said she felt as if an angel had touched her with a live coal.

The day Emma received the book, she and her sisters took it with them when they were sent to plant potatoes. They spent most of the day reading to each other and acting exciting scenes from the story.

"If I remember correctly," Emma told a reporter later, "the potatoes were not all planted."

Farm chores were left to Emma and her sisters because their only brother, Thomas, wasn't "quite right" and had spells, much to his father's disgust. It seems likely to us now that Thomas suffered from epilepsy.

When the girls came to the part of the story where Fanny cut off her brown curls, donned a man's jacket, and disguised herself as Seaman Channing, Emma shouted with joy and threw her straw hat high into the air. Still, she was disappointed to learn that Fanny disguised herself simply to rescue her lover. She pitied Fanny for having "no higher ambition than running after a man." Emma wasn't interested in love or sharing her own life with a man, especially with a man like her father, who was very strict and demanded that his wife and children obey him instantly, with no questions asked.

Emma grew to be a pretty girl. When young men came to call, she made it very clear that, unlike most farm girls, she wasn't in a hurry to marry. So naturally she was upset when her father ordered her to wed a man she didn't even like.

Emma's mother, who herself had married at age fifteen, agreed that Emma shouldn't be forced into this marriage. But Emma's father refused to listen. The older man had taken a liking to Emma, and Isaac insisted the wedding must take place. Emma's mother could see that arguing with her husband did no good. And while pretending to prepare for the wedding, she wrote to her good friend, Miss Annie Moffitt, who lived in Salisbury, and asked if she could use a young girl to help out in her hat shop. Miss Annie wrote back to say yes. A few weeks later she showed up at the farm, and when Isaac was busy in the fields, Annie and Emma rode off together in a horse-drawn carriage.

2

Salisbury, Hats, and Bibles

Emma found Salisbury, with its many shops and businesses, exciting, a lot more exciting than Magaguadavic had been. Mid-nineteenth-century Salisbury shops sold candles, woodenware and furniture, maple sugar, shoes and leather crafts, ready-to-wear clothing, and hats. Emma noticed, too, that not all businesses were run by men. Women in Salisbury owned dress shops and hat shops, and made soap, both plain and fancy. She could see that a woman living in Salisbury didn't need to marry just to survive. Emma decided that she, too, could make her own way in the world. Now she wore city store-bought dresses and learned to make and sell ladies' hats. Miss Annie taught her to copy the latest Paris fashions from magazines. Emma was a good saleslady, and easily convinced her customers that her creations were not at all too daring to wear to ladies' teas and church socials.

Emma wasn't interested in the young men who paid attention to her. She'd had enough trouble with her father and the older man in Magaguadavic, so she didn't feel like starting in with anyone new. She told all who asked that she "much preferred to earn her own living."

She became good friends with Henriette Perrigo, a

young woman who also made ladies' hats. Soon they opened their own hat shop in nearby Moncton and did quite well. Emma, at seventeen, seemed to be enjoying her independent life, and that's why people were stunned when she suddenly disappeared without saying a word to anyone, not even Henriette.

Even today, people aren't certain why Emma left Moncton so abruptly. Did she receive a letter from her mother, telling her that her father had discovered her whereabouts? Her mother had helped her escape from her father before; did Emma look for someone to help her now? Or did she decide then that no one could help her, and that she'd have to look out for herself? But she knew she couldn't keep running from town to town hoping to escape the unreasonable demands of her father. She'd have to think of some way to keep him from continually threatening her. Perhaps it was then that she remembered the adventures of Fanny Campbell in the favorite book of her childhood because, like Fanny Campbell, she cut off her curls, donned men's clothes, and disguised herself as a man. Her father would never be able to find her now.

Emma knew that disguising herself was risky. Pretending to be the opposite sex was against the law. Canadian judges declared that no one had the right to change God's plan. She knew that if she were discovered, she could be sent to jail, and when freed, perhaps forced once more to do her father's bidding.

Emma set out for Saint John, New Brunswick's biggest city. There, disguised as a man, she used the name Franklin Thompson, though most called her Frank. Emma was tall

Emma Edmonds as a man

and thin for a girl, and that helped. She tanned her face with stain, making it hard to see she didn't shave. She still needed to earn a living, and, of course, couldn't sell ladies' hats anymore. But there were lots of ads in the papers for book salesmen.

Emma sent for some samples of religious books from a publisher and studied them carefully. It took time for her to get her courage up. But finally, one evening at twilight, she knocked on a farmhouse door, introduced herself as Frank Thompson, Bible salesman, and made her first sale. Other sales came easier. Emma had grown up on a farm, so she knew how seriously farm families took religion. Her publisher, Mr. Hurlburt of Hurlburt and Company, Hartford, Connecticut, was pleased with his salesman. He claimed he'd employed book salesmen for thirty years, but never had one who could outsell Frank Thompson. Emma herself wrote, not modestly, "Such success I had deserves to be recorded in history." She earned good money, enough to buy her own horse and buggy, complete with a silver-mounted harness.

Still concerned about her disguise, Emma had a mole on her cheek removed, just in case someone thought Frank Thompson looked a lot like Emma Edmonds, the name she'd used in Moncton. In general, Emma was enjoying herself and had no desire to dress as a woman again. Men, she discovered, had much more freedom than women. As Frank Thompson, she ate in restaurants without needing a male escort, she could attend the theater by herself if she chose, and she could walk the streets alone late at night. No one cared what time Frank Thompson came home. But as Emma Edmonds, she never could have enjoyed such privileges.

Yet she found she couldn't totally escape her past, and in some ways didn't want to. Three years had passed since she'd seen her mother, and now she longed to see her again. She knew if she did return home for a visit, there was still the danger she could be recognized and sent to jail. Still, in October 1859, eighteen-year-old Emma decided to take the risk. Disguised as Frank, she headed for Magaguadavic.

She stopped at her married sister Frances's farmhouse first. Frances lived near her mother. Emma introduced herself as Frank Thompson, book salesman, and asked for something to eat. Frances studied her closely and said, "You may fool some people, but you can't fool me. I know who you are."

Emma admitted the truth and told Frances she wanted to visit their mother. Frances advised against it, saying Betsy had been seriously ill, and the shock of seeing Emma after so long might kill her. But Emma insisted, and Frances followed along. When they reached the family farm, Emma knocked on the door and introduced herself as Frank Thompson, Bible salesman. Betsy invited her in. They'd been visiting for about an hour when Betsy, her face drawn and her voice shaky, said to Frances, "Fanny, don't you think this young man looks like your poor sister?"

At that, Emma burst into tears, knelt at her mother's side and cried, "Mother dear, don't you know me?"

Betsy, puzzled, touched Emma's cheek softly, feeling for the telltale mole. Emma held her mother's hand and explained she'd had the mole removed. Then mother and daughter hugged, laughed, and cried, rocking one another in each other's arms.

Later Emma said to a reporter, "Oh, I tell you, we had a grand time there for an hour or two, and the big elder brother did not refuse to come in and rejoice over the prodigal's return."

Emma stayed in the family home as long as she dared, anxious to leave before her father returned from the fields. She had arrived by stagecoach, but now she learned that the train had been extended to Magaguadavic Siding, making her trip back to Saint John less difficult. Thomas accompanied her on the five-mile walk to the station. On the way they saw some partridges. Emma gave Thomas her shotgun, but Thomas, not being a good shot, missed. Emma took the gun, reloaded it, and when she spotted the partridges again, took aim and bagged six birds. She gave them to Thomas to take back home.

Stories about Emma's return to Magaguadavic vary. A niece of Emma's said she heard that Emma went directly to her mother's house and asked for something to eat, whereupon Betsy sent Thomas to Frances's for help in preparing the meal. Emma's niece said Frances recognized her immediately, but Emma begged, "Don't tell mother who I am." The truth is still uncertain, but it does seem almost unbelievable that Betsy would not recognize her own daughter, no matter how disguised. Perhaps Emma lied in telling of the event because later it was of utmost importance to her to prove that no one was able to recognize her, not even her very own mother.

—3—

War!

In the fall of 1860, Emma moved to the United States. She'd visited the United States at least once before to see her publisher, and perhaps found life there more exciting than life in New Brunswick, Canada. She stayed in Flint, Michigan, where she sold Bibles and religious books again. For a time, she boarded at the Pratt farm in nearby Oakland County. Lora Pratt, a young girl, wondered about Frank. She thought his features seemed too fine for a man, yet too coarse for a woman. When Lora's father told "Frank" that he handled a pitchfork like a woman, Emma explained she'd never done farm work before. But Elder Berry, who also boarded at the Pratts', was completely fooled. He and Emma became lifelong friends. He didn't learn the truth about Emma until many years later, when she told him so herself.

Emma moved back to Flint and boarded at the home of Thomas Jefferson Joslin, pastor of a local Methodist church. There she met Captain William R. Morse of the Flint Union Greys, soon to be Company F of the Second Michigan Volunteer Regiment. Later, to avoid confusion with the Confederates, who wore gray, the Union men would switch to blue. Damon Stewart, a clothing salesman and a good friend of Emma's, belonged to the Union Greys, and perhaps encouraged her to join. Many hoped war could still be averted, but thought the North needed to be ready, just in case. Emma, happy to be living in America, felt loyal to her adopted land. Still, she and many others were stunned the day they heard a newsman shout: "Fall of Fort Sumter—President's Proclamation—Call for 75,000 men!"

There was no turning back. This meant war. Emma knew she could flee to the safety of Canada, but she decided that would be cowardly, so she stayed in America. She returned her books to her publisher and told him she planned to join the United States Army.

Army medical exams were simple then, consisting of little more than a quick check of arms and legs, but Emma failed the exam. United States Army men had to be at least five feet eight and one quarter inches tall. Emma was only five foot six. She was disappointed when Damon and others she knew marched off without her. Then, in the middle of May, Captain Morse returned to Flint, looking for more recruits. Emma hurried to enlist again. This time the army wasn't so choosy.

According to Emma's account, a recruiting officer studied her hand closely, perhaps wondering why it seemed less masculine than others he'd seen.

"What sort of living has this hand earned?" he asked.

"Well, up to the present," Emma said, "that hand has been chiefly engaged in getting an education."

The officer believed her story and passed her on.

On May 25, 1861, Emma became Private Thompson, United States Army nurse. Damon was glad to see his old buddy once more.

Farm life had made Emma strong, and she did well in basic training. After drilling nine hours a day, she was no more tired than other soldiers. And unlike city-bred men, she was right at home handling firearms. Sometimes the men teased her about her small boots and called her "our little woman," since she was smaller and more delicately built than the others. But it was said in fun, and no one questioned Frank seriously.

On June 6 her unit headed for Washington. Emma was glad that, once the fighting began, she would not be sitting in some comfortable hospital fanning patients after a surgeon dressed their wounds. In her book, *Nurse and Spy*, she wrote proudly, "I was to go to the front and participate in all the excitement of the battle scenes, or in other words, be a 'Field Nurse.'"

Her regiment bivouacked at Washington Heights. Soldiers had their own small tents they sometimes joined together. Damon and Emma were bunk mates. Later Damon said he never knew his young bunk mate was female. Men slept in their clothes, and now that the weather was warm, they bathed in nearby lakes and streams. Emma took her baths alone and at night. Toilet conditions were primitive and foul-smelling, usually just a thirty-foot trench and pole, or rail, known as a sink. Emma wasn't the only one to handle personal needs privately.

Emma's day began at 5:00 A.M. with roll call. Sick call

followed. Then the men, in small groups, took turns making breakfast for one another. The army supplied bacon, hardtack (a hard, thick, breadlike cracker), and coffee beans. Soldiers hammered the beans with the butt end of their rifles, threw the coffee into boiling water, and added sugar. Some fancier cooks softened the hardtack with bacon drippings to give it more flavor.

Soldiers drilled twice daily. Blisters and sore feet were common. Regulation army shoes had square toes, left and right shoes identical.

Emma drilled, did her share of police duty, was detailed to help build roads and fortifications, stood guard, and in general faithfully performed her duties. She was well liked. After the war, Colonel Frederick Schneider remembered Frank as being dependable and conscientious. Damon said Frank showed good common sense.

Fighting hadn't begun yet, but still, many soldiers were sick, some suffering from sunstroke due to drilling long hours in Washington's heat. There was no general army hospital then, just temporary hospitals set up in hotels, schools, churches, and mansions. Emma's job was to visit these hospitals, helping out the best she could.

Hospitals filled up fast. Emma was upset that patients had to wait long hours before being seen by the few available surgeons. Food for the sick was inadequate, too, so she, along with Kate, the wife of a chaplain whom Emma referred to as Mr. B., took matters into their own hands. They visited the homes of fashionable ladies in Washington and Georgetown and begged for food and donations. A doctor also gave them some supplies. Soon their horse-drawn ambulance was filled with groceries, lemon syrup, jellies, ice, blackberry wine, and brandy. "What a change those little delicacies wrought upon our poor sick boys," she wrote.

In June, typhoid fever raged among the men. One soldier who lay dying of typhoid fever told his nurse, "I was sick when I joined the army, but I had no one to look after me. I knew the army would take care of me and let me die in peace." Caring for sick and disabled men who were ill when they entered the army became such a problem that later the War Department punished surgeons for not examining men more carefully.

Emma's work began in earnest. Hospital tents were erected in the shadiest part of camp. The ground was leveled and covered with boards or rubber blankets. In the center of each tent stood a table with books, medicines, and supplies. Four nurses took care of the immediate needs of the patients, working six-hour shifts without rest.

Emma's interest in nursing had begun years before while tending her brother Thomas when he had spells. Because she liked nursing, she was happy to be caring for those in need once again. She wrote in her journal,

> The nurses are usually very kind to the sick, and when off duty in the hospital spend much of their time digging drains around the tents, planting evergreens, and putting up awnings, all of which add much to the coolness and comfort of the hospital. Draining the grounds is a very important part of hospital duty, for when those terrible thunderstorms

come, which are so frequent in the south, it is morally impossible to keep the tent floors from being flooded, unless there are drains all around the tents. Great excitement prevails in camp at those tempests—the rain comes down in torrents, while the wind blows a hurricane—lifting the tents from the ground, and throwing everything into confusion. I have seen a dozen men stand for hours around one hospital, holding down the ropes and tent poles to prevent the sick from being exposed to the raging elements.

Emma's writing shows how dangerous weather and disease was to soldiers, just as dangerous as gunfire would be once the shooting began.

Emma worked closely with Orderly Sergeant Schneider, later promoted to Colonel. (In future wars it was rare if not impossible for a sergeant to become a colonel.) Emma also worked with William Shakespeare of Company K and Albert E. Cowles of Lansing, who had charge of supplies for the brigade hospital. Years later these men would remember working with Frank. All declared they'd had no idea Frank Thompson was really a woman.

During Emma's time off, she toured Washington with Kate. No one is certain if Emma let Kate and Mr. B. in on her secret. She might have thought that best, since otherwise the chaplain might not have been too pleased at his wife's close friendship with an army private.

The capital was becoming an armed camp. Weapons were piled high in official buildings, even in the White House itself. Soldiers by the thousands poured into Washington from every loyal state in the Union, ready to defend their country at a moment's notice. Soldiers jammed the streets, drilling and bugling in what had been, until recently, quiet neighborhoods. White army tents dotted surrounding hillsides. Emma viewed the scene with pride, eagerly anticipating "the day when that mighty host would advance upon the enemy, and like an overwhelming torrent sweep rebellion from the land."

—4—

Lieutenant James V.

Love came to Emma when she met tall, handsome Lieutenant James V., who had dark, curly hair and large black eyes. She said she'd known him before in Canada, although James didn't seem to recognize her.

"When we met in the army we met as strangers," she wrote in her nineteenth-century style. "The changes which five years had wrought, and the costume which I wore, together with change of name, rendered it impossible for him to recognize me. I was glad that he did not, and took peculiar pleasure in remaining unrecognized. We became acquainted again, and a new friendship sprang up, which was very pleasant, at least to me."

Emma was hiding her true emotions; when she said she found their new friendship "very pleasant," she was no doubt downplaying her feelings of love for the lieutenant.

"He was not an American," she wrote, "but was born of English parents, and was a native of Saint John, New Brunswick. I had known him almost from childhood, and found him always a faithful friend. . . . He had neither wife, mother, nor sister, and, like myself, was a wanderer from his native land. There was a strong bond of sympathy existing between us, for we both believed that duty called us there, and were willing to lay down even life itself, if need be, in this glorious cause."

But who was Lieutenant James V.? Was he Lieutenant James Varney, a clergyman who also served as a picket, guarding the camp? Or could he have been James A. Varney of the Seventh Maine, who had trained near the Second Michigan at Camp Winfield Scott? Emma was always careful to conceal the identity of those close to her, so perhaps her love wasn't a Canadian as she claimed, nor V. his real initial.

But there was no time now to think of romance. On July 15 her regiment received its orders. In two days it would be on its way to Bull Run, a stream near Manassas Junction in Virginia, about twenty-five miles from Washington and site of the first major battle of the war.

"Oh, what excitement and enthusiasm that order produced," Emma wrote. "Nothing could be heard but the wild cheering of the men as regiment after regiment received their orders. The possibility of a defeat never seemed to enter the mind of any."

When battle plans were announced, Washingtonians grew excited. Hundreds of local citizens, senators, and other public officials planned to watch the mighty Union army teach those Rebels a lesson.

The plan was that Federal armies, marching in three almost parallel columns, would seize Confederate outposts at Fairfax, sixteen miles from Washington, and at Centerville, five miles beyond. A third column would strike southward, forcing the Confederates to abandon Manassas Junction. Then people in Washington could rest easier.

Emma was released from her hospital duties. She was to travel to Bull Run along with her regiment. The sick in camp were tenderly put into ambulances pulled by horses and sent to Washington. Emma said her good-byes to the patients. "Oh, how hard it was to part with those men with whom we had watched so many weary days and nights," she wrote. Finally the ambulances started, carrying the patients toward the city, "looking like a great funeral procession."

July 17 was a bright, sunny day, and Emma's regiment set out on its long march, a march observed by Confederate general Pierre G. T. Beauregard standing on high ground. The element of surprise was gone. Spies had warned the Confederates of the coming battle. But the soldiers' spirits were high. Army bands played patriotic songs. "On to Richmond!" the men shouted over and over again. But as Emma rode along, she felt out of touch with all the cheerfulness. Watching bayonets gleaming and flashing in the sun, she couldn't help but think that many who seemed so eager to meet the enemy now would not return to tell of their victory or defeat.

The march was disorderly. Men broke ranks, stopped to pick blackberries, and rested under shady trees. When ammunition seemed too heavy to carry, men emptied cartridge boxes into a ditch. They reached Fairfax late and camped for the night. The men were still cheerful, in spite of the day's heat. Some built fires and others searched for food, ransacking neighborhoods for milk, butter, eggs, and poultry. Even grazing cattle were not safe. Such raids were clearly against orders, and soldiers, when caught, were arrested. Yet the odor of steak cooking soon spread throughout the camp.

The next morning, after a quick breakfast, the march continued. Again the day was hot, and men began to drop from thirst, exhaustion, and the effects of the sun. Water was in short supply. Men who couldn't keep up were put in ambulances and sent back to Washington. Toward noon, volleys of musketry could be heard in the direction of the advance guard. Soldiers searched every field and building, checking for the enemy.

The troops were no longer enthusiastic. Several regiments had been issued new shoes the day before leaving camp, and now their feet were raw and blistered. Emma and Kate relieved the men's sufferings with bandages and ointment.

General Irvin McDowell thought his men were too exhausted to attack just yet. He sent General Daniel Tyler to observe and report back. At Centerville, surgeons were preparing for the coming battle by taking over several buildings, including a stone church, and setting them up to receive the wounded.

On July 20, the eve of the battle, Kate and Emma walked about camp, viewing the scene. Many soldiers were writing letters by the glimmering light of the camp fires. Some were reading their Bibles. Others sat about, talking in low tones. But most were stretched out on the ground, wrapped in blankets and fast asleep, not worrying about tomorrow.

Emma and Kate heard singing in a grove nearby and walked over.

"I recognize Willie's voice," said Kate. "This is his prayer-meeting night."

They listened to the dying tones of the hymn and then heard young Willie pray for victory. Emma said she felt refreshed.

The next day, Sunday, three Union divisions moved forward at 2:00 A.M. The plan was to attack at dawn. No drum or bugle sounded as column after column wound its way over green hills and through hazy valleys, the soft moonlight falling on long lines of shining steel. The divisions branched off near Bull Run, taking the road to their ordered positions. Daylight broke bright and clear. At mid-morning the roar of artillery announced that the battle had begun.

Washingtonians, anxious to watch, hurried along Centerville Road amid the soldiers. Many carried picnic baskets filled with delicacies and French wines. Some traveled in fancy carriages.

Emma and Kate were part of General Samuel P. Heintzelman's division and took their positions on the field.

Emma wrote:

I imagine now I see Mrs. B. as she stood there, looking as brave as possible, with her narrow-brimmed leghorn hat, black cloth riding habit, shortened to walking length by the use of a page [peg], a silver-mounted seven-shooter in her belt, a canteen of water swung over one shoulder and a flask of brandy over

35

the other, and a haversack with provisions, lint, bandages, adhesive plaster, etc. hanging by her side.

Chaplain B. sat upon his horse, looking as solemn as if standing face to face with the angel of death.

The first man Emma saw mortally wounded was a gunner. Emma lifted his head and recognized young Willie, who had led the prayer meeting the night before. Soon, stretcher-bearers carried him from the field.

A colonel rushed over, giving orders, and a shot whizzed close to his head. The shot stunned the colonel for a moment, but on recovering, shook his head, said, "rather close quarters," and rode away.

The battle raged. Nothing could be heard except the thunder of artillery, the clash of steel, and the continuous roar of musketry.

"Oh, what a scene for the bright sun of a holy Sabbath morning to shine upon!" Emma wrote. "Instead of the chiming of church bells calling us to the house of prayer, the Sabbath school, there was confusion, destruction, and death."

Emma was sent seven miles away to Centerville for a fresh supply of brandy. When she returned, the field was strewn with the wounded, dead, and dying. Kate was nowhere to be found and Emma worried she'd been killed. Then she saw her, galloping her horse, with about fifty canteens hanging from her saddle.

"Don't care for the wounded now," Kate cried. "The troops are dying of thirst and beginning to fall back."

Mr. B. rode up, too, and when they had gathered all the

canteens they could find from the field, the three headed toward the nearest spring, a mile away. In spite of enemy sharpshooters, they filled the canteens, returned to the field, and distributed them to the exhausted men. Then Emma and Kate continued working among the wounded.

Colonel James Cameron, brother of the U.S. secretary of war, dashed up and shouted, "Come on, boys, the Rebels are in full retreat!"

Then he fell, his heart pierced by a bullet.

There was no time to carry off the dead, so Emma folded the colonel's arms across his breast and closed his eyes and left him "in the cold embrace of death."

Canister and grapeshot screamed through the air, spraying men with iron balls. The wounded tossed their arms wildly, calling for help. Many lay bleeding; the ground was crimson. General Ambrose E. Burnside's brigade was being cut down like grass by Rebel batteries. His men were falling back, but just then Federal reinforcements arrived, and soon, in a sheet of flame, Rebel gunners staggered and fell, their guns silenced.

Union Captains Charles Griffin and James Ricketts were ordered forward, and the enemy was routed. The Confederates retreated, and the battle seemed almost won. But then some Confederate forces who had eluded the Yankees in the Shenandoah Valley arrived by rail. Captain Griffin saw them, but because the men wore blue, he thought they were Union men. Uniform colors weren't standardized in either army yet. But when Captain Griffin finally realized the approaching forces were Rebels, his commander rode up and shouted, "Don't fire. They are your supports."

"No, sir, they are Rebels," Captain Griffin replied.

"I tell you, they are your supports," said Major Barry.

And so, obeying orders, Captain Griffin turned his guns away. The Confederates fired on Union gunners. Men and horses fell.

More Confederates reached the scene and more Union batteries fell to Confederate hands. The Union retreat was orderly at first, but then panic-stricken Washington spectators, mingling with soldiers along Centerville Road, turned the retreat into a rout. An overturned wagon made things worse. Some officers raced ahead of their men, escaping however they could. Two colonels were seen riding one horse.

Heading north toward Washington

Emma and Kate headed toward Centerville, which was still in Union hands. They managed to reach the stone church, where they saw stacks of amputated limbs and dead bodies. While Emma tended young and dying soldiers, she couldn't help but think of their mothers and the sorrow they would soon endure. A poem she knew came to mind.

> Not on the tented field,
>   O terror-fronted war!
> Not on the battlefield,
>   All the bleeding victims are;
>
> But in the lowly homes
>   Where sorrow broods like death,
> And fast the mother's sobs
>   Rise with each quick-drawn breath.
>
> That dimmed eye, fainting close—
>   And she may not be nigh!
> 'Tis mothers die—O God!
>   'Tis but we mothers die.

Emma wasn't a mother, but she knew soldiers weren't the only ones who suffered in a war.

The wounded were certain they would be taken prisoner soon. They begged Emma to leave, since she wouldn't be allowed to do anything for them once the Rebels arrived. And so, after placing water within the reach of many, Emma left and headed north toward Washington.

5

Hospital Work

When news of the Union defeat reached other parts of the world, many thought that the war was over and that the Union had been dissolved. Horace Greeley, whose *New York Tribune* had once proclaimed ON TO RICHMOND! in banner headlines, now urged President Abraham Lincoln to make peace with the Confederates.

The North was in a state of shock. In *Nurse and Spy*, Emma quoted Captain Noyes of the Union to describe the Washington scene: "There were stragglers sneaking along through the mud inquiring for their regiments, wanderers driven by pickets, some with guns and some without, while everyone you met had a sleepy, downcast appearance and looked as if he would like to hide his head from all the world."

Barrooms and groggeries in Washington were filled to overflowing with officers and men. Discipline was forgotten. And in plain sight of Washington, the Confederate flag flew high over Munson's Hill.

Emma walked about Washington for hours, searching for missing friends. Measles, dysentery, and typhoid fever plagued soldiers. She visited temporary hospitals, taking care of her friends and others, writing letters for those too sick to write.

"The hospitals in Washington, Alexandria, and Georgetown were crowded with wounded, sick, discouraged soldiers," Emma wrote. "That extraordinary march from Bull Run, through rain, mud, and chagrin, did more toward filling the hospitals than did the battle itself."

Abraham Lincoln wasted no time. On the day following the disastrous battle, he sent a message to General George Brinton McClellan: "Circumstances make your presence here necessary. Come hither without delay."

McClellan arrived in Washington the following Friday. Hailed as the "Young Napoleon," he quickly began reorganizing the Division of Washington, now renamed the Army of the Potomac. Emma, an admirer of McClellan, affectionately nicknamed "Little Mac," wrote, "I think that even his enemies are willing to admit that there is no parallel case in history where there has been more tact, energy, and skill displayed in transforming a disorganized mob into an efficient and effective army, in fact, of bringing order out of confusion."

Less than two weeks after McClellan took command, Washington bars were cleared of soldiers. The men were either in jail or back at their posts.

Emma was assigned to a hospital. "Oh, what an amount of suffering I am called to witness every hour and every moment," she wrote, "yet it is strange that the sight of all this suffering and death does not affect me more. I am simply eyes, ears, hands, and feet. . . . There are great,

41

strong men dying all around me, and while I write there are three being carried past the window to the dead room."

Soldiers looked after sick friends, preparing food to tempt their appetites. Men visited the hospital several times a day, asking about their comrades. "And it is touching to see those men," she wrote, "with faces bronzed and stern, tenderly bending over the dying, while tears course down their sunburnt cheeks."

Graves were not neglected. Soldiers planted carefully cut sod and evergreens. Carved headboards told of affectionate remembrances of comrades. Emma said it was the strong and enduring friendships among soldiers and their spirit of self-sacrifice that made hospital work seem less tiring.

Emma tried to be cheerful when working among the sick, but if a man asked if he were dying, she felt it her duty to tell him the truth. In spite of the suffering she witnessed, Emma said she had many pleasant experiences working in that hospital. For some men she wrote letters, for others she read from a favorite book. Emma's comrades, remembering Frank later, said that he was especially attentive to the sick and seemed to have a special talent for nursing.

Emma often went to great lengths to please her patients. When a German soldier repeatedly declared he could eat nothing until Frank caught him some fresh fish, Emma set out, with hook, line, and bait, for Hunter's Creek, a mile and a half away. She came back with a monstrous eel. The German patient was delighted. "Dhat ish coot—dhat ish coot," he said. Happily the doctor let him eat some of the fish.

In September, Emma had a new commander, Colonel Orlando Metcalfe Poe, who was to play an important role in her life, although Emma didn't mention him in *Nurse and Spy*.

The Army of the Potomac began to look more warlike as military discipline improved. "It was a splendid sight to see those well-drilled troops on dress-parade or being reviewed by their gallant young commander, upon whose shoulders the 'stars' sat with so much grace and dignity," she wrote.

The Army of the Potomac had not been involved in any battles, but its lines pushed forward, and pickets who guarded the lines in both the Union and Confederate armies often patrolled in sight of one another. Only cornfields and peach orchards separated Union and Confederate pickets. Men fired at enemy pickets in spite of flags of truce and generals' orders that this terrible practice be stopped.

Emma's concern for pickets has led many to wonder if the clergyman-picket whose words she quoted in *Nurse and Spy* was indeed her sweetheart, Lieutenant James V.

"Often, too, these posts [the pickets'] are in thick woods, where the soldier stands alone, cut off from camp, cut off from his fellows, subject only to the harrassings of his own imagination and sense of danger. The shadows deepen into inky night; all objects around him, even the little birds that were his companions during the day, are gathered within the curtains of a hushed repose; but the soldier, with every nerve and faculty of his mind strained to the utmost tension of keenness and sensibility, speaks only in whispers; his fingers tighten around the stock of his musket as he leans forward to catch the sound of approaching footsteps, or in absence of danger, looks longingly up to the cold, gray sky, with its wealth of shining stars."

Emma ended her discussion of pickets with words that sound as if she had a special picket in mind: "Oh, how my heart has ached for those men; and it seemed to me that the persons and regiments in which I was most interested always had the most picket duty to perform."

The Army of the Potomac continued to grow. Thousands of new recruits arrived each week. But McClellan explained there would be no major campaign in Virginia for some time. Bull Run had been a disaster, he said, a disaster that would not be repeated. His plan was to get everything ready and then attack in an orderly fashion. That way, he claimed, victory would be assured. Emma felt proud to be serving under such a general, a general who cared more about the safety of his men than about his own fame and glory.

In late September, the Confederates abandoned Munson's Hill, their outpost closest to Washington. In October, they fell back even further. The Army of the Potomac occupied abandoned Confederate positions without having to fire a shot.

Pressure for an advance by McClellan began to mount. "Forward to Richmond" again became the cry of newspapers and politicians, a cry McClellan ignored. "I intend to be careful and do as well as possible," McClellan told President Lincoln. "Don't let them hurry me, is all I ask." In spite of public criticism, Emma and the men in the Army of the Potomac remained fiercely loyal to their general, ready to follow him anywhere if ever he gave the order.

McClellan hired Allan Pinkerton to serve as a detective. Pinkerton was exceptional at catching spies, but not as good at determining an accurate Confederate troop count. He advised his general that the Confederates around Washington were 150,000 strong, three times their actual number. Some say Pinkerton took rumors and gossip too seriously.

In November, General in Chief Winfield Scott retired, and President Lincoln appointed McClellan chief of all Federal armies in his place. Emma was pleased that President Lincoln appreciated McClellan's talents and that her general had moved up in the world.

McClellan and the Army of the Potomac settled down for the winter. Emma, with Company F, Second Michigan Volunteer Infantry, was at Camp Michigan in Virginia.

In late December McClellan, worn out from stress, overwork, and public pressure, fell ill, stricken with typhoid fever. The North and the 220,000-strong Army of the Potomac waited for him to recover, though some feared he might not.

To relieve men for more active duty, soldier-nurses were

being replaced by women now, although many thought it improper for women to nurse men they didn't know. Colonel Poe appointed Emma postman, and later postmaster for the entire brigade, facts she doesn't mention in her writings. Why didn't Emma say she was a postmaster? Did she have some personal reason, not stated in *Nurse and Spy*? As postman, Emma came into close contact with men from other companies, men who might have wondered about the beardless and delicately built soldier.

—— 6 ——
On to Richmond! (Again)

MᶜClellan recovered from his bout with typhoid fever. Soon President Lincoln, tired of McClellan's caution, ordered him to begin an offensive by February 22. McClellan responded with the Urbana plan. His armies would sail down Chesapeake Bay to the mouth of the Rappahannock River, which would force the Confederates to abandon Manassas to defend Richmond where McClellan expected to defeat them.

The plan didn't work, but McClellan had another plan. He hadn't wanted to move his troops south by land to Richmond because he thought that would bring on many full-scale battles. So still moving his armies by water, he wanted to land them at Union-held Fort Monroe, the tip of the Virginia Peninsula, and drive up the peninsula to reach Richmond, seventy miles away. President Lincoln reluctantly agreed, on the condition that McClellan would leave sufficient troops to guard the nation's heavily fortified capital, something McClellan didn't believe really necessary.

In the middle of March, President Lincoln removed McClellan as commander in chief of all Federal armies and let him concentrate solely on the peninsula campaign.

McClellan marched the main body of his army back to Alexandria. Captain William Morse of Company F wrote in his diary, "Left Alexandria 12m. on board *Vanderbilt* with company of the 37th (N.Y.) and our own Regt. Day beautiful."

Regiments were huddled together on board the *Vanderbilt*, leaving little room for movement or comfort. Emma wrote:

> As soon as each transport received its cargo of men, horses and provisions, it floated out into the stream, while another steamed up to the wharf in its place, until the whole fleet lay side by side, freighted with over a hundred-thousand human lives, and awaiting the signal to weigh anchor. . . . [E]verything being in readiness, the signal was given, and the whole fleet was soon moving in the direction of Fortress Monroe, with the Stars and Stripes floating from every masthead, and the music of national airs awakening the slumbering echoes as we swiftly glided over the quiet waters of the Potomac.

Four hundred ships and barges transported McClellan's army of 121,500 men, plus 14,592 animals, 1,150 wagons, 44 batteries of artillery, 74 ambulances, pontoon bridges, and the mountains of equipment needed to sustain the army.

Emma was fascinated to see the *Monitor*, "the wonder of the age," lying off Fort Monroe. The *Monitor* was built in answer to the Confederate armor-plated *Merrimac*, which had dangerously threatened the North's superior naval power and blockade of Southern ports. In *Nurse and Spy* Emma wrote a detailed description of the miracle ship, ending with, "Many suppose the *Monitor* to be merely an iron-clad vessel with a turret; but there are, in fact, between thirty and forty patentable inventions upon her, and the turret is by no means the most important one. Very properly, what these inventions are is not proclaimed to the public."

The *Vanderbilt* arrived at Fort Monroe in drenching rain. The troops then proceeded to Hampton, once a beautiful village, but now a blackened mass of ruins, having been burned by the Rebels.

"It was a great relief to the troops to disembark from the filthy, crowded transports, notwithstanding they had to march through the mud and rain, and then pitch their tents on the wet ground," Emma wrote. "Fires were soon built, coffee made, and nice fresh bread served out, which was brought to us by the commissary department at the fort."

Late one stormy night, the whole camp was aroused when about forty escaped slaves approached the picket line and begged to be allowed to stay. Blacks who came under the protection of the United States Army were called contrabands, dating from the time when three black slaves working on Confederate fortifications escaped and asked protection from the United States Army. The slaves' southern master wanted the men returned, but Union General Benjamin F. Butler, a staunch abolitionist, refused. "I shall hold these Negroes as contraband of war," he said. General

Butler justified his action by saying that, if returned, the blacks would be put to work aiding the enemy. The term *contraband* stuck.

These particular blacks entering Emma's camp said they'd been sold down South, to prevent them from fleeing to the protection of the Union army. When Union soldiers learned they hadn't eaten in two days, they built a fire and served them hot coffee, bread, and meat. Blankets were brought in and soon the group seemed more comfortable. As Emma walked back to her tent she thought of the Will Jones resolve:

> Resolved, although my brother be a slave,
>   And poor and black, he is my brother
>   still;
> Can I, o'er trampled "institutions," save
>   That brother from the chain and lash,
> I will.

Emma, a white woman from Canada, had little contact with black Americans, but personal freedom was tremendously important to her. Wasn't the search for personal freedom the reason she'd first run away? Hadn't she, too, felt like a slave when forced to do her father's bidding? Perhaps it was the plight of the slaves in the South that had partly determined her loyalty to the North.

The rain continued for days, and the camp, according to Emma, "became a fair specimen of 'Virginia mud.'" Emma felt ill, certain it was vapors from nearby swamps and marshes that had made her sick. Many people then believed "bad air" caused illness and disease. As Emma lay in her tent, roasting one minute and shivering the next, she spent her time watching mule teams that passed nearby. Emma loved animals and, sick as she was, delighted in watching the antics of the mules.

Soon "On to Richmond" echoed through the camp, and the army was on the move again. Soldiers left with only two days' rations. Continuous rain soaked the claylike soil, and the two-day, twenty-three-mile journey on the road to Yorktown was slow and difficult. Wagons sank deep into the mud. In one tall tale, a mule was said to have sunk into the mud up to its ears, although the story claimed it wasn't a very big mule.

When soldiers arrived in front of Yorktown, they camped on ground over which water ran like a flood. By the fifth day, food wagons still hadn't arrived. The men were fiercely hungry. Food was delayed because the supply train was unable to travel on the water-soaked road. Emma said that it was the first time she'd ever witnessed a scarcity of food in the army. Horses, too, were in great need. Emma and some men went begging from local citizens. When they returned with biscuits, pies, and corn bread, they smelled steak cooking. At first, Emma and her friends thought the supply train had gotten through. They learned that instead "a dash had been made on some cattle." Emma, watching soldiers' reactions to the food situation, wrote:

> There was the selfish man, only intent upon serving himself, fearing there would not enough come to his share to satisfy his wants; then there was old churlish Nabal away by himself building a fire for his own

51

especial benefit, and which "no man dare approach unto." . . . There, too, was the cheerful happy man, who had been several hours engaged in cutting up and serving out to others, and had no lot or part in the broiled steaks which were smoking around him. . . . [T]hen there was another phase of character—one who always made it the first duty, under all circumstances, to look after those who were not able to look after themselves.

One day Emma went off alone on a food-hunting expedition. She stopped at an isolated farmhouse. The farm appeared to be in good condition, with cornfields flourishing, as if there were no such thing as a war going on in the land.

She rode up to the house, hitched her horse to a post, and rang the bell. A stately woman answered the door. The woman was well dressed, wearing black. She looked to Emma as if she belonged to the FFV, the First Families of Virginia.

"To what fortunate circumstance am I to attribute the pleasure of this unexpected call?" the woman asked.

Emma explained why she had come, not overlooking the fact that the woman seemed very nervous. The woman asked Emma to wait in another room while she prepared the food. Emma refused, deciding instead to keep a close eye on the Confederate woman. The woman walked about the kitchen in a stately manner, accomplishing little. Emma felt sure the woman was detaining her for some reason. Finally she asked if the things were ready yet.

"Oh, I did not know you were in a hurry," the woman answered. "I was waiting for the boys to come and catch some chickens for you."

"And pray, madam, where are the boys?" Emma asked.

"Oh, not far from here," the woman said vaguely.

"Well, I have decided not to wait," Emma said. "You will please not detain me any longer."

The woman's hands trembled as she packed some butter and eggs and put them into Emma's basket. Emma offered her a greenback, but the woman refused to take the money. Emma thanked her, and the woman followed her out.

Emma placed the basket on top of the post where her horse had been hitched, took her seat in the saddle, rode up and reached for her basket. She said good morning and once more thanked the woman for her kindness. She turned to ride away. Her instincts told her to keep her head low and forward on her horse's neck.

She had hardly gone any distance when a shot rang out. A ball passed over her head. Emma turned her horse and grasped her revolver. The woman fired a second time, but this bullet went wide of its mark. Emma held her seven-shooter in her hand, not certain where to aim. She didn't want to kill the woman, but she did intend to wound her. Emma fired, sending a ball through the palm of the woman's left hand. The woman shrieked and fell to the ground.

Emma dismounted, took the woman's pistol, and put it in her belt. She told the woman that if she uttered a sound she'd be dead. The woman wildly explained that within the last three weeks she'd lost her father, husband, and two brothers who had been sharpshooters in the Confed-

In search of food

erate army. She said Emma was the first Yankee she'd seen
after the death of her dear relatives. She said she was truly
penitent, and begged Emma not to turn her over to military
authorities.

Just then, Emma said later, she remembered the words
of the Savior: "If thy brother (or sister) sin against thee,
and repent, forgive him," so she bound the woman's hand
and brought her to camp to have her wound dressed properly by a doctor. Emma and the woman refused to answer
any questions, and since the woman, whom Emma called
Nellie, was shot by a Yankee, the surgeon had to care for
her.

Finally provisions arrived, and Emma's unit moved on

to a camp where there was more wood and less water, "adding much to the comfort of the troops."

Emma said that one of the most exciting incidents she ever witnessed occurred in front of Yorktown when General Fitz-John Porter climbed into a tethered balloon used by the Yankees to spy on Confederates. Unfortunately, this time the cable broke, sending the balloon adrift. Emma wrote poetically in *Nurse and Spy*, "All eyes were turned toward the receding car where General Porter sat in his aerial castle, being borne heavenward as fast as if on eagle wings, without the power either to check or guide his upward flight."

Directions were shouted from below: "Open the valve, climb up—reach the valve rope—the valve—the valve," people yelled, but it was impossible for the general to hear them. Pulling the valve rope would release gas from an envelope on top of the balloon, allowing the balloon to sail back down.

Finally the Signal Corps went into action, relaying instructions to General Porter with flags and a special alphabet system. Then the general was seen "looking no bigger than a spider" climbing up to reach the valve rope. He was unsuccessful. The balloon sailed over enemy territory. Shots were heard, fired from below, but too far away to reach the balloon. When the balloon sailed over friendly territory once more, the general tried to reach the valve cord again. This time he was successful. He pulled it and landed safely on top of a Yankee tent, which probably saved him from serious injury.

7

Becoming a Spy

Emma was serving as postman at Camp Winfield Scott in front of Yorktown. She galloped her horse twenty-five miles to Fort Monroe to pick up bushels of letters, papers, and packages, no easy task. Roads were muddy and progress was slow. Often she slept by the side of the road, next to her horse. Emma didn't flinch when she learned that another postman, traveling the same route, had been killed. When next she rode, she heard the rustling of papers beneath her horse's hooves and knew she was traveling the very spot where that postman had met his death.

On Sunday, April 13, 1862, Captain Morse wrote, "In camp in front of Yorktown. Day beautiful and everything quiet on the lines. Mail came, first in a week. . . ."

One day, when Emma returned from a mail pickup, she found the camp quiet and almost deserted. Soldiers were just returning from the burial of a comrade.

Emma was devastated when she learned that the soldier was none other than her beloved Lieutenant James V. Brokenhearted, she wrote, "My friend! They had buried him, and I had not seen him! I went to my tent without uttering a word. I felt as if it could not be possible that what I heard was true. It must be someone else. I did not inquire how, when, or where he had been killed, but there I sat with tearless eyes."

Mr. B. told her that James had been struck by a deadly minié ball (a powerful type of rifle bullet) at the picket line and killed instantly.

"Without shroud or coffin, wrapped in his blanket, his body was committed to the cold ground," Emma wrote. "They made his grave under a beautiful pear tree, in full bloom, where he sleeps peacefully, notwithstanding the roar of cannon and the din of battle which peal forth their funeral notes over his dreamless bed."

Emma found comfort in a poem:

> One more buried,
>   Beneath the sod,
> One more standing
>   Before his God.
>
> We should not weep
>   That he has gone;
> With us 'tis night,
>   With him 'tis morn.

Emma couldn't sleep that night. She expressed her grief by writing:

Visions of a pale face with a mass of black wavy hair, matted with gore which oozed from a dark purple spot on the temple, haunted me. I rose up quietly and passed out into the open air. The cool night breeze felt grateful to my burning brow. . . . The solemn grandeur of the heavens, the silent stars looking lovingly down upon that little heaped mound of earth, the deathlike stillness of the hour, only broken by the occasional booming of the enemy's cannon, all combined to make the scene awfully impressive. . . . It was there, in that midnight hour, kneeling beside the grave of him who was very dear to me, that I vowed to avenge the death of that Christian hero.

Emma said she could now understand Nellie's feelings when she'd fired her pistol at her.

In *Nurse and Spy*, Emma said she lost interest in nursing then, although she was actually a postman at the time. She said she discussed wanting to do something else with Kate and her husband, and the chaplain said he knew of a dangerous situation he could get for her if she had enough courage: A Federal spy had been captured and hanged, and someone was needed to replace him. Emma said that Mr. B. urged her to think the matter over carefully. She answered that she was not afraid of death, that her life was in the hands of the Creator and that his will would be done.

Why did Emma decide to do something as dangerous as spying? Did she spy to avenge James's death? Or was her real reason the one she gave years later? She said then she wanted to spy because she was naturally fond of adventure.

Emma went to the War Department in Washington and was ushered into a room where she was questioned closely by Generals Samuel P. Heintzelman and Thomas F. Meagher. What were her thoughts about the rebellion, the generals asked, and why was she willing to do such dangerous work? The generals were pleased with Emma's answers, and Frank Thompson passed trial number one.

Next Emma displayed her knowledge of firearms. "I sustained my character worthy of a veteran," she wrote immodestly.

Then she was once more cross-examined, this time by a committee of high-ranking military experts. Last came the examination of the bumps of her skull to see if her organs of secretness and combativeness were developed well enough for spying. People then believed the shape of the skull was determined by the brain beneath, where various traits were thought to be situated. Emma passed that examination, too, with flying colors. She claimed Mr. B. said he felt proud, since he was the one who had recommended her.

Emma took the Oath of Allegiance, as required, swearing her loyalty to the United States.

On her first spying mission, Emma pretended to be a black. Allan Pinkerton believed in spies masquerading as blacks. Blacks would realize a white Northerner was spying, Pinkerton said, but they wouldn't turn the white in because they wanted the North to win the war. Besides, blacks often worked on fortifications, and he needed information about Confederate construction sites.

Emma blackened her body, put on a "plantation suit" such as slaves commonly wore, shaved her head, and put on a curly, black wig. She left camp at 9:30 one night, and by midnight had slipped behind Rebel lines. Then she lay down on the cold, damp ground and rested as best she could.

In the morning, she made friends with some slaves carrying breakfast to Rebel pickets. Her new friends gave her a cup of hot coffee and some corn bread, and when they returned, she followed them into Yorktown. After reporting to some overseers, the slaves went to work on the fortifications. A Confederate officer noticed Emma standing about and asked why she wasn't working. Emma answered that she was a free black and on her way to Richmond to find work. Too late, she learned that had been the wrong thing to say. The officer called over the man in charge of the slaves and yelled, "Take that black rascal and set him to work, and if he don't work well, tie him up and give him twenty lashes, just to impress upon his mind that there's no free niggers here."

Emma was led to a place where about one hundred slaves were working. She was given a pickax, shovel, and an enormous wheelbarrow, and began doing the same work as the slaves. She shoveled gravel and wheeled her barrow up a narrow plank to the top of an eight-foot wall. The work was terribly hard even for strong men and few were able to wheel their barrows up alone. Helpful blacks kept her from falling off the plank. Before long, Emma's hands were covered with blisters. As the sun beat down, she began to sweat. She prayed her black stain wouldn't streak. She knew that if she were discovered, she'd get a lot worse than twenty lashes.

Emma saw that the food black workers ate was far different from the food served to white overseers and soldiers. The blacks had neither meat nor coffee, while the whites received both. Whiskey was served to the blacks and whites, but not enough to get people drunk or keep them from working. Emma stayed alert and listened carefully whenever soldiers and overseers discussed Confederate plans.

Work ended at night, and Emma was free to roam about the fortification. She managed to make out a brief report of the mounted guns she saw and made a rough sketch of the works, hiding the information in the lining of her shoe. She knew her hands would be in no condition to load and unload gravel the next day, so she found a black worker about her size who agreed to change places with her. All she'd have to do was supply water to thirsty soldiers.

The next day was cooler, so Emma didn't have to work hard. She stayed close to the soldiers, listening to their talk of Rebel plans.

On the evening of the third day, Emma was ordered to carry supper to some outer pickets. It was just the opportunity she'd been hoping for. When the night came, she slipped through the Rebel lines and headed toward her camp.

She reported to headquarters, removed as much of the dark stain from her skin as she could, and wrote: "I am naturally fond of adventure, a little ambitious and a good deal romantic, and this, together with my devotion to the Federal cause and determination to assist to the utmost of my ability in crushing the rebellion, made me forget the unpleasant times."

Still, Emma decided to let her hands heal before starting off on another adventure.

—8—

The Battle of Williamsburg

In the spring of 1862, President Lincoln and the politicians continued to pressure McClellan to attack, but McClellan remained cautious, convinced he was outnumbered. He learned from Washington that additional troops he'd been counting on would not be coming. And it seemed to him, too, that the Confederates were receiving reinforcements, although the reinforcements were just one of Confederate General John Bankhead Magruder's tricks. Magruder marched a column of his men in a circle, part of which was in Yankee sight. The Yankees counted the same few hundred men over and over again. And some of Magruder's guns, the Yankees learned later, weren't guns at all, just peeled logs painted black to look like cannons.

McClellan decided it was best to take Yorktown by siege. Siege warfare was slow, but it would save his men's lives.

Huge guns were brought up, partly by barge and partly over muck-filled land on which logs had been laid. Teams of one hundred horses and more pulled guns, some weighing ten tons. By May 3, 114 siege guns and 300 pieces of small artillery were in place. McClellan was at last ready to bombard Yorktown, beginning May 5. Emma wrote ominously:

The next day [May 4] the continuous roar of cannon all along the lines of the enemy was kept up incessantly. Nor did it cease at night, for when darkness settled over the encampment, from ramparts that stretched away from Yorktown there were constant gushes of flame, while heavy thunder rolled far away in the gloom.

But shortly after midnight the firing stopped. At dawn, McClellan learned that the Confederates had fled. The Confederates knew they were no match for McClellan's siege guns, so they headed for Richmond. McClellan won Yorktown without a fight.

"The news spread throughout the Federal army like lightning," Emma wrote. "Music and cheering were the first items in the programme, and then came the following order: 'Commandants of regiments will prepare to march with two days' rations, with the utmost dispatch. Leave and not return.' "

At about eight in the morning, the Union advance guard entered Yorktown. They pushed on, chasing the retreating Rebels. They marched in the pouring rain over a road Captain Morse claimed to be the worst road he had ever seen.

Fighting broke out in the evening, when Union cavalry caught up to the Confederate rear guard two miles from

Williamsburg. The fighting ended at night, but resumed the next morning.

Emma kept busy. "One moment I was ordered to the front with a musket in my hands," she wrote, "the next to mount a horse and carry an order to some general, and very often to take hold of a stretcher with some strong man and carry the wounded from the field."

There was one incident Emma would never forget: When a colonel fell, moaning, she rushed over. She and another soldier carried the colonel, a heavy man, a quarter mile to safety. The colonel moaned pitifully the whole way. Emma and her helper gently laid the stretcher down at the head surgeon's feet. Dr. Bonine spread a blanket on the ground, and the colonel was carefully placed upon it. There was no blood, but the colonel seemed in too much pain to say where he'd been wounded. So Dr. Bonine, a kind and gentle man, examined the colonel tenderly.

After the doctor had covered every inch of the colonel's body, he said at last, "Colonel, you are not wounded at all; you had better let these boys carry you back again."

The colonel became very angry. He rose to his feet and shouted, "Doctor, if I live to get out of this battle, I'll call you to account for those words."

"Sir, if you are not with your regiment in fifteen minutes," the doctor replied, "I shall report you to General Heintzelman."

Emma left in disgust. She decided that in the future she'd make certain a man was wounded before helping him.

By 4:00 P.M. the Federals had fallen back into the woods,

but General Philip Kearny arrived just in time with fresh troops and plunged them into battle.

Kearny, who had lost an arm in the Mexican War, never let his disability stand in his way. He held his sword in his right hand and the reins of his horse in his teeth and dashed through fire and smoke among the columns of his men, urging them on.

"Never lose a hand," he told his orderly. "It makes putting a glove on difficult."

In order to see where the enemy was hidden now, Kearny galloped out into the open field as if on parade. Immediately a storm of balls and bullets burst around him.

"Now you see, my boys, where to fire," he said. Knowing many of his men were facing gunfire for the first time, he spoke kindly: "Don't flinch, boys. They're shooting at me, not at you . . . That's it, boys. Go in, gaily."

One by one, Kearny's men retook batteries that had been lost, forcing the Confederates back.

Emma was nearby when Captain Morse's leg was shattered from his ankle to his knee. "Just carry me out of range of the guns," Captain Morse said, and then, pointing to some men who had fallen, added, "Go back and look after the boys. Perhaps they are worse off than I am."

Emma was touched by his words, but stayed with Captain Morse and helped carry him off the field. She rode with the captain in an ambulance. When the ambulance broke down, she and four other soldiers carried the wounded captain on a litter to Williamsburg Landing. The following morning, Emma watched while Captain Morse, in intense pain, was placed on a stretcher and then lifted by pulleys aboard a hospital transport and carried to a stateroom. Emma remained until she was certain the captain was as comfortable as possible.

Ever since knowing Captain Morse in Flint, Emma had admired him. True, he was a strict disciplinarian, but he was kind and considerate, too, never asking his men to do more than he was willing to do himself.

The Battle of Williamsburg, the first major Union victory, proved to the Federals, the Confederates, and the world that Northerners could fight and win. Fort Magruder was silenced and the Stars and Stripes floated on high, though losses had been heavy. The battle cost the Confederates 1,603 men killed, wounded, or missing. Federal casualties were greater: 2,239, including 456 killed. In Emma's regiment, one out of every five men was killed. The lines between the two armies were littered with dead and wounded men and horses. Weary soldiers carrying torches waded through mud, guiding horse-drawn ambulances around dead bodies so that they wouldn't be trampled upon. Later would come the sad job of identifying and burying the dead.

Confederate and Union wounded were moved to churches and college buildings. Union doctors and nurses treated patients from both armies with loving care.

Damon, Emma's good friend and bunk mate, was seriously wounded. He was to be sent home to Flint to recover. Emma and Damon said tearful goodbyes.

Colonel Poe wrote in a letter to his wife, "Many of our brave fellows were sent to their long home. It was an awful battle, awfully conducted, and if it had not been for a handful of Michigan men [Kearny's division] who threw themselves forward through the broken ranks of Hooker's division, the Army of the Potomac would not now be in existence. This fighting has never been surpassed in the world!"

Emma wrote dramatically, yet sincerely:

Oh, what a day was that in the history of my life, as well as thousands both North and South. It makes me shudder now while I recall its scenes.

O war, cruel war! Thou dost pierce the soul with untold sorrows, as well as thy bleeding victims with death. How many joyous hopes and bright prospects thou has made blasted; and how many hearts and homes hast thou made desolate. As we think of the great wave of woe and misery surging over the land, we cry out in very bitterness of soul—oh, God! how long, how long?

The Federals held the field. Ahead lay Richmond, only fifty miles away.

— 9 —

Spying Again

All eyes were on Richmond, the Confederate capital. Nashville and New Orleans had fallen. If Richmond fell, too, as the North hoped and the South feared, the war would be over, the North victorious.

McClellan moved up the peninsula slowly, so slowly that Kearny privately called him the Virginia Creeper.

The roads were bad. Emma said that in one instance it took them thirty-six hours to travel five miles. Plans had changed and the Union army was divided. Three corps were north of the Chickahominy River and two corps, including Emma's, lay south. In dry weather, the river was only about fifteen yards wide in most places, but wet weather could flood surrounding marshes for a mile. Now, the river was rising and had reached its highest level in twenty years. Most bridges had washed away. Only the Grapevine Bridge, secured by ropes and too dangerous to use, remained. Without bridges, the Federals would be unable to reach Richmond. Union engineers, constructing new bridges, worked feverishly in water waist deep and sometimes above their heads.

Did the Confederates know of the Union plight? Emma was sent spying to gather information.

This time she went as an Irish peddler-woman, selling pies and cakes to soldiers. Emma, disguised as a man, now pretended to be a woman. A natural-born mimic, she brushed up on her Irish brogue.

Since the new bridges weren't ready yet, she plunged her horse, Frank, into the cool waters of the Chickahominy River. When she reached shore, she gave Frank a pat and sent him back home, where a soldier waited to receive him. Emma didn't know the exact location of the enemy camp, so she decided to spend the night in the swamp. She planned to tell enemy pickets she was escaping from advancing Federals, a common excuse. Unfortunately, her peddler-woman costume and her cakes and pies got soaked on her trip across the river. She put on her wet costume and began to feel chilled. When night came, she covered herself with her damp patchwork quilt. Emma was certain that breathing in the miasmatic air of the swamp made her feel worse.

During the night she took turns freezing and burning with fever from ague. In the morning she felt no better. Her chills and fever lasted two days. On the third day she felt better, but was fiercely hungry. The day was gloomy, and after roaming about with no sun or compass to guide her, she realized she was hopelessly lost. Toward evening, she heard the booming of a cannon, "the sweetest and most soul-inspiring music that ever greeted my ear," she wrote. She turned in the direction of the cannon booms and walked out of the swamp.

When she came to a small white house, she peeked inside. The house seemed deserted except for a sick Rebel soldier she saw lying on a straw mattress. Emma entered the house and spoke gently to the soldier. The soldier's voice was weak. He said he'd been ill with typhoid fever and had managed to crawl to this house. There had been people living in the house then, he said, but they'd left in fear of the Yankees.

Since neither the soldier nor Emma had eaten for days, Emma went into the kitchen and searched for food. She found some cornmeal, kindled a fire, and within fifteen minutes made tea and had a hoecake baking.

Tending a dying Rebel

"I fed the poor famished Rebel as tenderly as if he had been my brother," Emma wrote, "and he seemed grateful for my kindness, and thanked me with as much politeness as if I had been Mrs. Jeff Davis. The next important item was to attend to the cravings of my own appetite, which I did without much ceremony."

After eating, Emma felt more comfortable and took a closer look at her Rebel patient, a tall man of about thirty, with dark hair and mournful hazel eyes.

"It is strange how sickness and disease disarm our antipathy and remove our prejudices," she wrote. "There before me lay the enemy of the Government. . . . he may have been the very man who took deadly aim at my friend and sent the cruel bullet through his temple; and yet, as I looked upon him in his hopeless condition . . . I looked upon him only as an unfortunate suffering man."

It was growing late, and Emma was anxious to find something she could use for a light. All she could find was a piece of salt pork, which she fried. She poured the fat into a dish in which she dipped a cotton rag. She lit the rag and soon had a respectable light. After making some cornmeal gruel for her patient, she screened the windows so that the light wouldn't attract the Rebels. She fastened the windows and doors of the building, preventing anyone from entering without her knowledge. She took her place beside her patient, where "the dews of death were already gathering on his pallid brow."

After a while the soldier asked, "Am I really dying?"

Emma said she regretted that so often she had to answer that awful question in the affirmative.

"Yes, you are dying, my friend," she said. "Is your peace made with God?"

The soldier said it was and then made a final request. He said his name was Allen Hall and told Emma his regiment. If she passed through the Confederate camp between here and Richmond, would she ask for Major McKee, give him his gold watch," and tell him I died peacefully"?

Emma promised she would.

"He was almost gone. I gave him some water, raised the window, and using my hat for a fan, I sat down and watched the last glimmering spark of light go out from those beautiful windows of the soul," Emma wrote in her dramatic style.

Allen Hall died at midnight. Emma closed his eyes. She folded his hands across his breast, drew a blanket close around him, and "left him in the silent embrace of death."

Emma, concerned about her readers' thoughts of how a woman should behave, wrote, "Perhaps some of my readers will pronounce me . . . entirely devoid of feeling, when I tell them that two hours after I wrapped the unconscious form of my late patient in his winding-sheet, I enveloped myself in my patchwork quilt and laid me down not far from the corpse, and slept soundly until six o'clock in the morning."

Emma cut a lock of hair from Allen Hall's temple, took his watch and a small package of letters from his pocket, replaced the blanket, and bade him farewell.

She ate quickly, then rummaged about the house and found some mustard, pepper, an old pair of green spectacles, and a bottle of red ink, and began to improve her disguise.

From the mustard she made a plaster and held it to one side of her face until her cheek blistered. She cut the blister open and put a black patch over it. Next she painted a red line around her eyes with the ink. She gave her pale complexion a tinge with some rouge she found in a closet. Then she put on the green glasses and pulled her hood down, covering her face a few inches.

Before leaving, she searched the house once more, this time looking for things an Irish peddler-woman would be likely to carry. She filled two baskets, being careful to hide her pistol.

Emma followed the road to Richmond for about five miles before she noticed anyone. When she saw a picket in the distance, she sat down to work on her disguise. She sprinkled black pepper on a handkerchief and held it to her eyes. She looked in the small mirror she always carried with her and felt pleased. "I perceived that my eyes had a fine tender expression, which added very much to the beauty of their red borders," she wrote.

Emma resumed her journey. She approached the picket and displayed a flag of truce, which she had made from a piece of cotton curtain in the house. The picket signaled her to come forward. Emma was pleased that the guard looked like a jolly Englishman and had a smile on his good-natured face. He questioned her briefly, and Emma told a sorrowful story. She held her peppered handkerchief to her eyes from time to time "and tears ran down my face without the least effort on my part," she wrote.

The guard listened sympathetically to her tale and allowed her to enter camp. Emma hadn't gone far when the guard called her back. He advised her not to stay in camp overnight. He said that one of their spies had just returned, saying the Yankees intended to attack either today or tonight.

"But Jackson and Lee are ready for them," he said, telling Emma how many masked batteries the Rebels had prepared. He pointed to a brush heap. "There is one that will give them fits if they come this way."

Emma hurried to find Major McKee, but learned he wouldn't return until evening, so while waiting, she wandered about camp, gathering information.

Major McKee returned at five o'clock. Emma gave him Allen Hall's gold watch and papers and told him how the young man had died.

"You are a faithful woman, and you shall be rewarded," the major said.

He gave her a ten-dollar bill, promising more after Allen Hall's body was recovered. Emma thanked him, but refused the money. The major looked puzzled, and Emma realized nervously that he was no doubt wondering why a poor woman was refusing money, so before he became too suspicious, she blurted in her best Irish brogue, "Oh, Gineral, forgive me! but me conshins wud niver give me pace in this world nor in the nixt, if I wud take money for carrying the dyin missage for that swate boy that's dead and gone—God rest his soul."

The major seemed satisfied and told her to wait until he returned with some men. When he came back, Emma asked for a horse, saying she'd been sick and couldn't walk so far twice in one day. The major ordered a horse and a young black servant helped Emma mount.

"Now, boys, bring back the body of Captain Hall, even if you have to walk through Yankee blood to the knees."

Emma wrote that, until that moment, she hadn't known Allen Hall was an officer. Since officers in both armies held positions of responsibility, their welfare was generally treated with great concern and respect.

Emma and the men made their way cautiously, not wanting to risk being discovered by Yankees who might be hiding. When they reached the house, a sergeant asked Emma to ride on ahead to see if Yankees were coming and report back.

"I turned and rode slowly down the road," Emma wrote, "but not seeing or hearing anything of the Yankees, I thought it best to keep on in that direction until I did."

Emma kept the horse and named him Reb. She reported her findings to the Federals, omitting mention of the Confederate sergeant and his escort, permitting them to return to their camp unmolested, "bearing with them the remains of their beloved captain." Union officials were pleased. There was no doubt about it, Frank Thompson had done a fine job impersonating a woman, so fine that there began to be talk. Could this small, slight soldier actually be a woman?

— 10 —

A Horse Called Reb

The next day, new orders were issued: "Upon advancing beyond the Chickahominy the troops will go prepared for battle at a moment's notice. . . ." General Fitz-John Porter attacked the Confederates, clearing a path for reinforcements McClellan hoped would arrive.

"The battle at Hanover Courthouse was certainly a splendid affair," Emma wrote, "and a very important victory to the Army of the Potomac."

But three days later a fearful storm broke. Rain came down in torrents, so much so that the weather reminded Emma of the great flood in the Bible, when "the fountains of the great deep were broken up and the windows of heaven were opened."

The Rebels welcomed the rain. Many believed the incessant rains were being sent by God to help them destroy the Yankees. The Confederates attacked McClellan's forces south of the Chickahominy, certain they couldn't be reinforced from across the river.

The Battle of Fair Oaks, also known as Seven Pines, began at 1:00 in the afternoon, May 31. It seemed to

On the battlefield

Emma, who was serving as General Kearny's orderly, that the Rebels were bent on total annihilation of the Yankees. Federal reinforcements had been sent for, but so far none had arrived. Kearny reined his horse abruptly, scribbled a note on an envelope, and thrust it into Emma's hands.

"In the name of God," the note read, "bring your command to our relief, if you have to swim to get here—or we are lost."

"Go as fast as your horse will carry you to General G. . . ." Kearny ordered.

Emma raced Reb at top speed and then plunged him into the river and swam him across. Emma says she was ordered to find General G., but more likely it was General McClellan she was ordered to find. McClellan sent General Edwin V. Sumner into action. Sumner, nicknamed Bull of the Woods because of his booming voice, made his way toward the one remaining bridge. Engineers warned that the Grapevine Bridge was too dangerous to use, but Sumner ignored their words and marched his men across.

"The eager, excited troops dashed into water waist deep and, getting upon floating planks, went pouring over in massive columns," Emma wrote.

Many soldiers reached shore safely. Then the moorings of the Grapevine Bridge pulled loose, and the bridge floated away, preventing more soldiers from crossing.

Emma was back on the field when a ball struck General Oliver O. Howard in the arm. She leaped from Reb and hitched him to a stump. She ripped open the general's sleeve, gave him water to drink, and then poured some water on his arm to cool the wound. When she went to her saddlebags to get some bandages, Reb dug his teeth into her arm, tearing her flesh almost to the bone. Then Reb turned and kicked her, throwing her several yards away. Her arm swelled quickly, and soon she was almost as badly off as the general, but she continued to perform her duties.

Emma was ordered to a sawmill where soldiers went to have their wounds dressed and be out of danger. She was told to inform all who were able, including the surgeons and hospital corps, to come to the front.

Emma put the vicious Reb in a nearby building where there was plenty of hay and corn, but didn't unsaddle him. She examined her sore arm and discovered it was worse

A hospital tree

than she had thought. In one place her flesh hung by small shreds. Yet her arm was not her only problem. Her side, where Reb had kicked her, was badly bruised and felt lame. But she decided that this was not the time to complain, so she said to her pain, "Stay thou here while I go yonder." With her good arm, she bound her wounded arm in a sling, then went about tending the soldiers.

She had no scissors or knives, so she used her teeth to tear off stiffened, blood-soaked, thick woolen uniforms from soldiers. She needed bandages, but she didn't dare go near Reb and her saddlebags. Instead, she thought she'd try her luck at nearby houses. Before leaving, she went among the wounded and found two men who could stand well enough to cool wounds with water and relieve soldiers' thirst.

She had no luck at the first house nor at the second. She was in hostile territory where most didn't think kindly of Yankees. When she came to the next house, she drew her pistols and demanded cotton, new or old, sheets, pillow-caes, or anything that could be used for bandages. A man answered the door. When he saw her pistols, he trembled from head to foot. He called his wife, who demanded five dollars for an old sheet, two pillowcases, and three yards of new cotton cloth, an outrageous price at that time. Emma paid the woman three dollars in change, took the supplies, and left.

Emma was on her way back to the sawmill when she discovered that her sore arm was bleeding badly, probably from grasping one of her pistols. She felt weak and dizzy and sat down by the side of the road to rest. She was relieved when she saw a horseman in the distance and rejoiced when the man turned out to be a chaplain. The chaplain came closer, looked at Emma a moment, then rode to the other side of the road and continued on his way. Emma was disappointed, but she said she still felt relieved knowing that a chaplain would be assisting the wounded back at the sawmill.

Emma returned to the sawmill, tore up the cotton, and bandaged as many wounded soldiers as she could. She looked about for the chaplain and discovered him wrapped in a blanket, sleeping on some hay, as if there were no suffering in the world, and no wounded men nearby. Emma wrote:

> Oh, how I wanted to go to him, quietly lay my hand on him and say, "Chaplain, will you be so kind as to take the saddle from my horse? It has been on since early morning, and I am not able to take it off." Not that I cared particularly for having the saddle removed, but just for the sake of having Reb bring the chaplain to his senses, and give him a little shaking up, so that he might realize that these were war times, and that consequently it was out of the question for chaplains in the army, especially in time of battle, to:
>
> > Be carried to the skies
> >   On flowery beds of ease;
> > While others fought to win the prize,
> >   And sailed through bloody seas.
>
> But instead of doing so, I sat down and wept bitter tears of disappointment and sorrow.

Clearly, Emma's army experiences were affecting her deeply. Still, she fared better than General Howard, whose right arm had to be amputated above the elbow.

Emma turned Reb over to General Kearny, telling him the horse was not safe to ride. The general, doubtful, patted Reb and checked his limbs.

"He is certainly a splendid horse," Kearny said according to Emma, "and worth three hundred dollars of anyone's money. All he requires is kind treatment, and he will be as gentle as anyone could desire."

But when Kearny turned his back, Reb kicked him. After a few more kicks, Emma said Kearny became convinced that "Reb's social qualities were somewhat deficient, his bump of combativeness largely developed, and his gymnastics quite impressive."

Emma, in a joking mood, hadn't forgotten when the bumps on her own skull had been felt to see if her organs were well-developed enough for spying.

— Ⅲ —

Another James

On June 3, McClellan issued a statement to his troops: "Soldiers of the Army of the Potomac! I have fulfilled at least part of my promise to you. You are now face to face with the Rebels, who are held at bay in front of their capital. The final and decisive battle is at hand. . . ."

While the weather still held McClellan in check, Emma received a leave of absence. She needed time to let her arm and side heal. She went to Williamsburg and visited Union and Rebel hospitals. Next she went to Yorktown to see the camp where she had spent so many weeks. She found the spot, "undisturbed, away in the corner of the peach orchard, under an isolated pear tree, a heaped-up mound, underneath which rested the noble form of Lieutenant V. It was sweet to me to visit this spot once more," she wrote. "I knew that in all probability it would be the last time; at least for a long period, perhaps forever." Again, Emma found comfort in poetry:

84

When this frail body shall be done
  with earth,
And this heart shall be free from
  care;
When my spirit enters that other
  world,
Oh, say, shall I know thee there?

But why did Emma say she would not be visiting James's grave again? Was it because she had a new love now, another James? Sergeant James Joseph Reid, a six foot three, blue-eyed Scotsman, served in the Seventy-ninth Regiment, New York Militia, General Kearny's division in the Army of the Potomac. His regiment had trained next to hers back at Camp Winfield Scott, early in the war. James had been captured at Bull Run and then released in a prisoner exchange. Perhaps his prison experiences had aroused Emma's sympathies.

Emma grew restless wandering about, so she headed back to camp and, maybe, to James.

McClellan continued preparing for his final advance on Richmond. Emma said that soldiers were cheerful, knowing that soon "they would walk the streets of Richmond triumphantly, to reap the fruits of this summer's campaign."

Yet there were delays. On June 4 McClellan wrote, "I dare not risk this army . . . I must make a sure thing of it." On the 10th he complained, "We have another rainstorm on our hands."

Yet, an advance guard came to within four miles of the city. In quiet hours Union soldiers heard Richmond clocks chiming the hours.

People in Richmond were panic-stricken. The Confederate legislature voted to burn the city rather than let it fall into enemy hands. Treasury gold was crated, ready to be boarded on a train kept under steam. President Jefferson Davis sent his wife and children to Raleigh, North Carolinia, for safety.

But Confederate General Robert E. Lee was more aggressive than McClellan. Now reinforced by General Stonewall Jackson, Lee attacked Union troops, and a series of battles, known as the Seven Days' Battles, began.

Emma didn't do any spying at this time. She spent her time attending soldiers in temporary hospitals.

Emma was at the Battle of Malvern Hill, the last of the Seven Days' Battles. Although not insensitive to the suffering of the soldiers, she couldn't help but be awed by the sights she saw:

> The battle of Malvern Hill presented, by far, the most sublime spectacle I ever witnessed. All the batteries I had seen before, and those which I have seen since, were nothing to be compared to it. The elevated position which the army occupied, the concentration of such an immense force in so small compass, such a quantity of artillery on those hills all in operation at the same time, the reflection of the flashes of fire from hundreds of guns upon the dense cloud of smoke which hung suspended in the heavens, turning it into a pillar of fire which reminded one

of the camp of the Israelites [and] of God's dealings with His people of old, the vivid flashes of lightning, the terrific peals of thunder mingled with the continuous blaze of musketry, sudden explosions of shell and the deafening roar of cannon, combined to make a scene which was awfully grand. My soul was filled with the sublimity and grandeur of the scene, notwithstanding the ghastly wounds and piteous groans of the mangled, helpless men around me. Thus it continued from seven to nine in the evening, the most thrilling picture which the imagination can conceive.

The Battle of Malvern Hill was a Union victory, but during the Seven Days' Battles, the Federals had been driven back. Now, instead of advancing to Richmond, as originally planned, McClellan decided to retreat.

Kearny was furious when he received the order. At headquarters, he begged permission to make an attack at once. He said that he and Hooker could march straight into Richmond. But McClellan insisted the retreat must take place. A staff officer who was present reported that Kearny then denounced McClellan "in language so strong that all who heard it expected he would be placed under arrest until a general court martial could be held."

But McClellan, apparently used to Kearny's outbursts, listened and did nothing. McClellan's plans were carried out, and with the retreat all hope of a short war ended.

President Lincoln and Northern citizens were disappointed with McClellan's failure to take Richmond, and none seemed impressed by the masterful strategy it took to move cannons and horses, mules and wagons, trophies and battle flags, farm hands, shopmen, and ditch diggers, soldiers and supplies, in a line stretching out for miles, to a place of safety at Harrison's Landing on the James River.

Emma remained loyal to her general, agreeing that it was the lack of reinforcements that caused the failure of the most recent campaign. Pinkerton had again told McClellan he was vastly outnumbered, when in fact the Army of the Potomac outnumbered the Confederates. McClellan said he planned to return and move on Richmond once he had sufficient troops and supplies.

About a week after the troops reached Harrison's Landing, Emma received a request to come to Colonel Hansen's headquarters. Colonel Hansen was the officer Emma had helped carry off the field at Williamsburg and whom Dr. Bonine had threatened to report unless he returned to his regiment. Following the battle, the colonel managed to get his hometown newspaper to print his version of his role at Williamsburg:

> Colonel Hansen was severely wounded at the Battle of Williamsburg while gallantly leading a desperate charge on the enemy's works, and was carried from the field, but no sooner had the surgeons bound up his wound than the noble and patriotic colonel returned again to his command and led his men again and again upon the foe until the day was won, when he sank upon the ground, exhausted from loss of blood and fatigue, and was carried the second time by his men from the field.

When Dr. Bonine heard about the article, he wrote to the newspaper advising them of the facts.

Now the colonel spoke to Emma excitedly. "I am informed that you are one of the persons who carried me off the field when I was wounded at Williamsburg and witnessed the infamous conduct of Dr. E. [Bonine] and heard the insulting language he used toward me."

When Emma didn't answer, the colonel grabbed her roughly. "See here, boy, what do you mean?" he asked. "Why do you not answer me?"

"Pardon me, sir," Emma said, "I was not aware that you asked me a direct question. I understood you to say that you were informed that I was one of the persons who carried you off the battlefield at Williamsburg. I have the honor to inform you that thus far, your information was correct."

"Then you saw the treatment which I received and heard the abusive language Dr. E. made use of on that occasion?"

"I saw Dr. E. examine you carefully and thoroughly, and when he could discover no cause for your being brought there, I heard him say, 'Colonel, you are not wounded at all. You had better let those boys carry you back to your regiment;' and when you suddenly recovered your strength you sprang to your feet, making use of threats and profane language, he said: 'If you do not return to your regiment within fifteen minutes I will report you to General [Heintzelman].'

The colonel relaxed his grip on Emma's arm, and then spoke in a gentler manner. He handed Emma a paper and asked her to sign it, promising a reward if she did.

Emma read: "Colonel Hansen has been infamously treated and maliciously slandered by Dr. E. while said colonel was suffering from a wound received at Williamsburg battle. Two of the undersigned carried him bleeding from the field and witnessed the cruel treatment and insulting language of Dr. E."

After reading, Emma said calmly, "Colonel, I must decline signing this paper." Ending the interview, she touched her hat in a mock salute and left.

At about that time, the *Wolverine Citizen* of Flint, Michigan, printed a letter from F. H. Rankin: "The health of the regiment is kept very good by the care of Dr. Bonine and his assistants, who are ever on the alert for any nuisance that causes disease. . . ."

Actually health conditions in both armies were anything but good. Doctors then didn't know why wounds became infected or what caused disease. Pus, oozing from a wound and called "laudable pus," was thought to be part of the healing process and an encouraging sign. Surgical dressings weren't sterilized and surgical tools rarely even rinsed between operations in the field.

Typhoid fever, dysentery, pneumonia, and tuberculosis were killers. No one knew what caused these illnesses or how to cure them. Little was known about sanitation, either, or about how to maintain a safe water supply. About 220,000 soldiers in the Union army died of disease, a fifth of whom never even saw battle.

Emma went to Washington again, visiting hospitals and delivering messages from friends and others. She found the military scene there astonishing. She was used to seeing generals at camp dressed casually in fatigue coats, often without even a star to show their rank. But in Washington, generals wore plumed hats, scarlet-lined riding coats, swords and sashes, high boots and Spanish spurs, immense epaulets, and glittering stars. Even their horses were decorated.

In spite of the troubled times, Emma said that people in Washington seemed quite cheerful, except "during the reign of terror, when some bold dash of rebel cavalry is made upon the devoted city, and then there is a genuine panic for a short time."

Emma visited the Senate chamber, which was empty "except for a few specimens of young America who were playing leapfrog over seats and desks." Then she went to view the picture galleries. Next she stopped at the Soldiers' Free Library, which had 2,500 books of historical, biographical, and religious works, available to soldiers both in and out of hospitals. Emma, a Canadian by birth, knew little about America's history, so she was anxious to learn about George Washington, Pocahontas, Captain John Smith, and other American heroes.

Emma stopped by a contraband camp, where she said former slaves seemed happy in their new freedom. A Northern woman she met at the camp said she'd come to Washington to nurse sick soldiers, but instead had decided to teach blacks to read and write. The woman said she loved her work and found the blacks eager to learn.

Emma was curious to learn from former slaves how they

felt about their new situation, and spoke to one who seemed willing to answer questions. "How is it with you? Do you think you can take care of yourself, now that you have no master to look after you?" she asked.

"Gosh, guess I can," the man answered. "Been taking care of self, and master, too, for fifteen years. Guess I can take care of this nig all alone now."

Back at Harrison's Landing, Emma spent most of her time working in hospitals. "In our own hospital," she wrote, "we generally managed to assort and arrange the patients [so] as to have all of the same temperament and disease together, so that we knew just what to do and what to say to suit each department. We had our patients divided into three classes; one was our working department, another our pleasure department, and a third our pathetic department. One we visited with bandages, plasters, and pins; another, with books and flowers; and the third with beef tea, currant wine, and general consolation."

Emma often watched the patients while they slept and thought she could then judge their characters better than when the men were awake. She wrote:

Some faces would grow stern and grim. They were evidently dreaming of the war, and living over again those terrible battles in which they so recently participated; some groaned over their wounds, and cursed the Rebels vigorously; others grew sad . . . Often the roughest grew young and pleasant when sleep smoothed away the hard lines from the brow, letting the real nature assert itself. Many times I would be quite disappointed, for the faces which looked merry and pleasing when awake would suddenly grow dark and hideous, as if communing with some dark spirits of another world.

One poor fellow, whose brain was injured more than his body, would wear himself out more in an hour when asleep than in a whole day when awake. His imagination would conjure up the wildest fantasies; one moment he was cheering on his men, the next he was hurrying them back again, then counting the dead around him, while an incessant stream of shouts, whispered warnings, and broken lamentations would escape from his lips.

McClellan wanted to move on Richmond again, but President Lincoln informed him that the troops he demanded were simply not there, so the order came to evacuate Harrison's Landing.

"None knew whither they were going," Emma wrote, but it was clear they would not be advancing back toward Richmond as hoped, "to avenge the blood of their fallen comrades."

── 12 ──

A Most Unusual Soldier

Soldiers set out for Fort Monroe, Yorktown, and Newport News to board transports to Aquia Creek and Alexandria to support General John Pope's newly formed Army of Virginia. (Robert E. Lee's Confederate army was called the Army of Northern Virginia.) Emma's destination was Newport News, seventy miles away. She rode with the chaplain and Kate, Dr. Bonine and his wife, and possibly James, since her memories of that time seem so happy. She wrote that they "made up a small party, independent of military discipline, and rode fast or slow, just as it suited our fancy, called at the farmhouses and bought refreshments when we were hungry, and had a good time generally." But on one occasion they had an experience that could have ended in disaster.

The group stopped at a farmhouse to sleep, but Emma said she grew suspicious of the man of the house. He closed doors behind him too carefully to suit Emma and moved about in a nervous manner. Emma was certain Rebel soldiers were hiding somewhere in the house. Pretending to go for a short ride, she raced to the provost marshal for help. (A provost marshal was assigned to each military district to maintain order. He functioned like the police.) The provost marshal assigned a corporal and six men to go with Emma. The men searched the house and found four Confederate soldiers plus two officers who said they were sons of the family and home on furlough. The soldiers claimed to be ill, but Dr. Bonine examined them and said they were just as healthy as he was. The provost guard marched the men to headquarters. Emma and her small group decided to spend the night closer to the main army, where they would be safer.

The army marched on until it reached transports heading for Aquia Creek. At Aquia Creek, troops were immediately ordered to Alexandria. The Army of the Potomac was broken up and men sent to serve under new commanders. General McClellan was ordered to Washington with only his staff to command. Some soldiers were sent to assist General John Pope, but Emma went spying.

This time Emma disguised herself as a female contraband and traveled with several former slaves who said they preferred living with their families in bondage to living free without them. These blacks had found Northerners to be cold and unfriendly. They missed their relatives and longed to be with them again, even if it meant being enslaved.

"I had no difficulty whatever in getting along," Emma wrote, "for I, with several others, was ordered to headquarters to cook rations enough, the Rebels said, to last them until they reached Washington."

Disguised as a woman

After a few hours, Emma managed to obtain the information she'd been sent to get. From a general and his staff, she learned the number of troops at several important points and when they were expected to arrive. The following morning, while helping at breakfast, she removed a coat from a stool that was in her way. When the coat fell, some papers "accidentally" slipped out. She put them in her pocket and hurried back to her tent. She left while breakfast was being served and delivered the documents to Federal authorities. The papers contained orders to different corps commanders, with instructions on how and when to move.

Emma's pose as a female was convincing, so convincing that again gossip circulated that Frank Thompson might actually be female. If her generals believed the gossip, it didn't prevent them from sending Frank out on more spying assignments.

"During those battles and skirmishes of Pope's memorable campaign," she wrote, "I visited the Rebel generals three times at their own camp fires, within a period of ten days, and came away with valuable information, unsuspected and unmolested."

On September 2, Emma and the soldiers received good news. Little Mac was back. Divisions were being reorganized, and once more McClellan would be commander of the Army of the Potomac. Soldiers threw their caps high in the air, danced, and frolicked like schoolboys.

Emma didn't mention Colonel Poe in *Nurse and Spy*, but on September 16, he wrote a note to his wife: "Staying in Washington over the time given in my pass. I made no explanation until after I was released from arrest, when I explained how it happened that I stayed there, and all was again harmonious and happy." What was his explanation? Many have wondered about Emma's true relationship with Colonel Poe. Was he simply her commander and nothing more? Or were they romantically involved? Some have even suggested that the colonel might have spent some of his time in Washington with Emma.

Emma was at the Battle of Antietam, one of the bloodiest of the war. While working among the wounded who had been moved to a safer place, Emma noticed "the pale, sweet face of a youthful soldier," severely wounded in the neck.

Emma wrote, "The wound bled profusely, and the boy was growing faint from loss of blood. I stooped down and asked him if there was anything he would like to have done for him. The soldier turned a pair of beautiful, clear, intelligent eyes upon me for a moment . . . and said faintly, 'Yes, yes; there is something to be done, and that quickly, for I am dying.'"

Emma hurried to find a surgeon, who told her that nothing could save the soldier.

"I administered a little brandy and water to strengthen the wounded boy," Emma continued, "for he evidently wished to tell me something that was on his mind before

Tending a female soldier

he died. The little trembling hand beckoned me closer, and I knelt down beside him and bent my head. . . . I listened with breathless attention. . . . "

" 'I can trust you, and will tell you a secret,' the boy said. 'I am not what I seem, but a female. I enlisted from the purest motives, and have remained undiscovered and unsuspected. I have neither father, mother, nor sister. My only brother was killed today. . . . I shall soon be with him. . . . I wish you to bury me with your own hands, that none may know after my death that I am other than what I appear.' "

Then, looking at Emma intently, the soldier said, "I know I can trust you—you will do as I requested?"

Emma assured the soldier that she would do as asked.

Did the soldier trust her because she realized Emma was a woman, too?

Emma found a chaplain who prayed with the soldier. She stayed until the soldier died, an hour later.

"Then, making a grave for her under the shadow of a mulberry tree," she wrote, "near the battlefield, apart from all the others, with the assistance of two boys who were detailed to bury the dead, I carried her remains to that lonely spot and gave her a soldier's burial, without coffin or shroud, only a blanket for a winding-sheet. There she sleeps in that beautiful forest, where the soft southern breezes sigh mournfully through the foliage, and the little birds sing sweetly above her grave."

Again Emma used poetry to express her feelings. Perhaps it was the fact that the soldier was a woman that filled her with such deep emotion.

Her race is run. In Southern clime
   She rests among the brave;
Where perfumed blossoms gently fall,
   Like tears, around her grave.

No loving friends are near to weep
   Or plant bright flowers there;
But birdlings chant a requiem sweet,
   And strangers breathe a prayer.

She sleeps in peace; yes sweetly sleeps,
   Her sorrows all are o'er;
With her the storms of life are past:
   She's found the heavenly shore.

Surely Emma must have wondered about herself at that time. Would there be some kind soul to bury her, too, in secret, if she were killed? James Reid knew the truth about her, of course, but what would happen if her sex became common knowledge? Would men who were simply good friends be accused of having illicit relationships with her?

Once when she was riding a mule, the mule plunged into a ditch, and she injured her side in the fall. Her friends, Richard Halsted and Sam Houlton, then delivered the mail for her. Sam had brought soothing remedies for her bruises. Robert Bostwick had brought meals to her tent. Would Richard, Sam, Robert and others be falsely accused if her sex were discovered? Perhaps some men did know Emma's true identity; still, fear of discovery by others did keep her from receiving the medical care she needed.

She frequently coughed up blood now—due to her fall from the mule and other mishaps, she supposed—but she didn't dare consult a doctor.

In spite of her health problems and the pain and suffering of others that she witnessed constantly, Emma said she managed to enjoy army life, and wrote: "I would not have my readers think that camp life in the army is so very unpleasant after all, for I have spent some of the pleasantest, happiest hours of my life in camp, and I think thousands can give the same testimony."

Emma compared army life to life in the city, giving us a feeling of what living in the mid-nineteenth century must have been like:

> Our candles are not brilliant; but the sight of the lights of the camps all around is more pleasant than the glare of the city gas. The air is the pure air of heaven, not the choky stuff of the metropolis. The men are doing something noble, not dawdling away these glorious days in selling tape and ribbons. The soldier lives to some purpose, and if he dies, it is a hero's death. The silks of that wealthy mart may be coveted by some; but what are the whole to our bullet-riddled old flag, which passed from the stiffening hands of one color-bearer to another, in the days of many a battle?

By her words, Emma showed how touched she was by the courage and patriotism of the soldiers, and today, when we hear so much talk about the pollution in our cities, it's interesting to note that Emma, writing more than 100 years ago, meant pollution, too, when she wrote of "the choky stuff of the metropolis."

The casualties at the Battle of Antietam were devastating: over 22,000 men killed or wounded on both sides. McClellan was shaken by the sufferings of his men and decided not to follow up his victory by attacking further. He ignored President Lincoln's order to destroy Lee's army. The next day the battlefield remained relatively quiet, and Lee and his army escaped south to Virginia.

— 13 —

Slaughter at Fredericksburg

W hile the Army of the Potomac remained inactive, Emma visited Harper's Ferry, where in 1859 John Brown had been tried, convicted, and hanged for seizing a Federal armory and inciting slaves to rebel. To Emma's joy, she discovered that John Brown had not been forgotten. She listened with delight as soldiers walked about singing "His soul goes marching on."

She viewed the courthouse where John Brown's trial had been held. In the judge's chair now sat an abolitionist preacher.

"Oh! If John Brown had only lived to see that day!" Emma wrote, showing her sympathy for Emancipation and her distaste for slavery.

Emma was back with her regiment by October and back to her duties as mail carrier. On the 15th Colonel Poe wrote to his wife, "I am very busy—twenty persons waiting to transact business, and I can't write much, for Thompson is awaiting to carry this to Washington."

*　　*　　*

In late October, bridges were completed at Harper's Ferry, and the Ninth Corps, to which Emma's Second Michigan Regiment was attached, advanced slowly into Virginia—too slowly to suit McClellan's critics. The Ninth Corps occupied Lovettsville, a pretty village that Emma said reminded her of New England. She wrote: "The army was in admirable condition and fine spirits and enjoyed this march exceedingly, scarcely a man dropping out of the ranks for any reason whatsoever. . . . As the army marched rapidly over the country from village to village . . . many thrilling adventures occurred . . . and one which came very near [to] being my last. . . ."

The third day after leaving Lovettsville, Emma was sent to McClellan's headquarters on an errand. She was told the headquarters was about twelve miles toward the rear. To help her travel quickly, she left her food and personal belongings in an ambulance. After riding several miles, no one could tell her where McClellan's headquarters was located. At about noon, she learned his headquarters was six miles away, though she had to ride ten miles to get there. She delivered her messages, managed to get her horse fed, and then tried to get some food for herself, but failed. She approached some private homes. The people at the homes told her "they had not a mouthful in the house cooked or uncooked—but of course I believed as much of that story as I pleased," she wrote.

The day had been cold, with a few showers, and now it started to snow, "a sort of sleet which froze as fast as it fell. This was an October day in Old Virginia."

Traveling at 10:00 P.M., Emma was hungry, wet, and

shivering. She hoped to catch up to the troops she'd left in the morning. But, unknown to her, their route had been changed due to some skirmishes with Rebel guerrillas, and so she was riding in the wrong direction. Eventually she came upon some newly enlisted troops on their way to join McClellan. The men had been put on guard duty without definite orders. Officers had decided to remain where they were until the main column arrived. Emma wrote:

As I rode up, one of the boys—for if a boy he was, not more than sixteen summers had graced his youthful brow—stepped out in the middle of the road with his musket as at "trail arms" and there he stood till I came up close to him, and then he did not even say "halt," but quietly told me that I could not go any farther in that direction. Why not? Well, he didn't exactly know, but he was put there on guard, and he supposed it was to prevent any one from going forward or backward. Whether they have the countersign or not? Well, he did not know how that was. I then asked him if the officer of the guard had given him the countersign. Yes, but he did not know whether it was right or not.

"Well," said I, "perhaps I can tell you whether it is correct; I have just come from headquarters." He seemed to think that there could be no harm in telling me . . . so he told me without any hesitation. Whereupon I proceeded to tell him the impropriety of doing so; that it was a military offense for which he could be punished severely; and that he had no right to give the countersign to any one, not even the general in command. Then [I] told him how to hold his musket when he challenged anyone on his beat, and within how many paces to let them approach him before halting them, etc. The boy received both lecture and instructions "in the spirit of meekness," and by the time I had finished, a number of the men were standing around me, eager to ask questions. . . .

Her conversation shows how capable she'd become.

Emma rode on. She thought she'd stop at a village she came to, but learned enemy guerrillas occupied it, so she kept on traveling until two in the morning "when my horse began to show signs of giving out." She stopped at a farmhouse, but couldn't get anyone to hear her:

I hitched my horse under cover of a woodshed; taking the blanket from under the saddle, I lay down beside him, the saddle blanket being my only covering. The storm had ceased, but the night was intensely cold, and the snow was about two or three inches deep. I shall always believe that I would have perished that night, had not my faithful horse lain down beside me, and by the heat of his beautiful head, which he laid across my shoulders (a thing which he always did whenever I lay down where he could reach me), kept me from perishing in my wet clothes.

Emma had started at daylight the previous morning and had not eaten in twenty-four hours. Her horse had only eaten once. She had ridden all day and almost all night in a storm. In the morning her hands and feet were numb and she could hardly stand. But when daylight came, she set out again. After a mile, she came to a field where un-husked corn stood in stacks, and she fed her horse. When some Union cavalry approached, she let them know she was hungry, and they fed her breakfast from their hav-ersacks. Afterward she rode along with the cavalry, who were searching for guerrillas.

The guerrillas surprised them and killed two of their men. Emma's horse received three bullets. The horse reared and plunged before he fell, throwing Emma to the ground.

"My horse fell beside me," she wrote, "his blood pouring from three wounds. Making a desperate effort to rise, he groaned once, fell back, and throwing his neck across my body, he saturated me from head to foot with his blood. He died in a few minutes."

Emma remained on the ground, motionless, pretending to be dead because the guerrillas were still in sight. She saw them search the pockets of the two dead soldiers, but by a stroke of good luck, they left her alone.

When reinforcements arrived, Emma returned to camp with a soldier who let her ride his horse while he walked.

"After returning to camp," Emma wrote, "I found that I had sustained more injury by my fall from the horse than I had realized at the time. But a broken limb would have been borne cheerfully, if I could only have had my pet horse again."

*   *   *

After the Battle of Antietam, President Lincoln had urged McClellan to advance against Lee before the Confederates could be reinforced. If McClellan moved quickly on Lee, he could force Lee out into the open for a fight to the finish. But even after crossing the Potomac into Virginia, McClellan headed toward Richmond slowly. Finally, in November, President Lincoln lost patience and relieved McClellan of his command, ending the general's army career. Emma considered that terrible news and wrote: " 'Father Abraham' took the favorable opportunity of relieving the idol of the Army of the Potomac from his command . . . just as he was entering upon another campaign, with his army in splendid condition."

At McClellan's farewell address, the men cheered their general until they were hoarse. Mixed among the cheers were curses at his leaving. There was talk that the general might disobey the order, march to Washington with his army, and demand to be reinstated, but McClellan apparently had no such plans.

Why was the Army of the Potomac so loyal to McClellan? Perhaps it was because McClellan was such an able organizer. Discipline in his army was good. His men were well fed and never lacked clothing and supplies. Then, too, McClellan's defensive activities, so troublesome to politicians and the public, spared soldiers' lives. Casualties in the Army of the Potomac, with McClellan in command, stayed low.

Emma, disappointed at McClellan's leaving, wrote: "That was a sad day for the Army of the Potomac. The new commander [General Ambrose E. Burnside] marched the army immediately to Falmouth, opposite Fredericksburg. Of the incidents of that march I know nothing, for I went to Washington."

Emma often went to Washington when she needed time to recover from an injury. But perhaps this time she went to soothe her low spirits as well.

Emma visited her old battlefields, where she saw "men and horses thrown together in heaps, some clay thrown on them above ground; others lay where they had fallen, their limbs bleaching in the sun, without the appearance of burial.

"There was one in particular," she wrote, "a cavalryman: He and his horse both lay together; nothing but the bones and clothing remained, but one of his arms stood straight up, or rather the bones and the coat sleeve; his hand dropped off at the wrist and lay on the ground; not a finger or joint was separated, but the hand was perfect."

Emma heard some tales almost too horrible to believe, yet a clergyman said they were true. He claimed that in one town, Rebel soldiers sold Yankee skulls for ten dollars apiece. She heard, too, that it was not unusual for Rebel women to wear rings and jewelry made from Yankee bones. She wrote, "This to me was a far more sickening sight than was presented at the time of the battles, with dead and wounded lying in their gore."

Emma went from Washington to Aquia Creek and then on horseback to Falmouth, where she found the army encamped in mud for miles along the Rappahannock River.

On December 3 Colonel Poe wrote to Nelly, his wife, "Frank Thompson (mail carrier) has just returned from Washington. He brought me a pocket full of apples and doughnuts, and a very nice orange."

Two days later Colonel Poe issued an order: "Private Frank Thompson, Company F, Second Michigan Volunteers, is detailed on special duty at these headquarters as postmaster and mail carrier for the brigade."

Often when Emma was listed as postmaster, she was serving as a spy or was sent out on some special assignment, though perhaps at this time she really was working as a postmaster. References like these, though, offer proof of Emma's activities.

"All the mud and bad roads on the peninsula could not bear the least comparison with that of Falmouth and along the Rappahannock," she wrote. It was December and very cold, but constant rains kept the roads in a deplorable condition.

On December 11 the Federals shelled Fredericksburg, considered by General Burnside to be a barrier to the Union march on Richmond. Engineers laid bridges in the midst of showers of bullets from Rebels hidden in buildings and rifle pits, but still they worked steadily. Two out of every three engineers working on the bridges were either killed or wounded. "But as fast as one fell, another took his place," Emma wrote.

Finally Federals rowed across the river, and in house-to-house fighting cleared out the snipers. Then Union regiments moved in and occupied the town. But again Federal forces moved too slowly. When they advanced toward low-lying hills beyond Fredericksburg on December 13, they discovered the hills were now well defended by the Confederates.

On the battlefield at Fredericksburg, Emma served as orderly to Poe, who had been promoted to general. She entered in her journal, "While I write, the roar of cannon and musketry is almost deafening, and shot and shell are falling fast on all sides. This may be my last entry in this journal. God's will be done. I commit myself to him, soul and body. I must close. General H. [Poe] has mounted his horse, and says Come!"

Emma said she saw many strange sights during that battle. Never before had she seen a soldier deliberately shoot himself with his own pistol in order to prevent the Rebels from doing so.

As one brigade was ordered into battle, she saw another officer shoot himself through the side—"Not mortally, I am sorry to say," she wrote, "but just sufficient to unfit him for duty; so he was carried to the rear—and he protesting that it was done by accident."

That night, Emma rode three miles with General Poe to General William B. Franklin's headquarters at Fredericksburg, which Emma said was the darkest of any night she could recall. On the way, they passed General George D. Bayard, a general of the cavalry, drinking a cup of coffee under a tree, his headquarters. When they returned, the general was dead, struck by a stray bullet.

Emma said she only left her saddle once in twelve hours,

and that was to assist an officer who lay writhing in agony from cramps and spasms. After she gave him some strong medicine to quell his cramps, the officer mounted his horse and rode off.

Emma was sent to Church Hospital to find Doctor Bonine. An immense shell had fallen in the building among the wounded and dying. The shell did not explode or injure anyone and was carried out and laid among newly amputated limbs, limbs that had just recently been in contact with "such instruments of death."

On one of her rides, Emma passed a graveyard where a group of soldiers were praying, "strengthening their souls for the coming conflict . . . with a marble slab for an altar." Emma, deeply religious, was always quick to note soldiers at prayer.

Because of her great riding skill, she was in constant demand, carrying messages in the midst of heavy fire with a fearlessness that brought praise from many officers. Major Byron M. Cutcheon of the Twentieth Michigan Regiment declared later that he never would forget Frank's bravery during that battle.

But Emma was filled with disgust for the slaughter at Fredericksburg and wrote:

Of course it is not for me to say whose fault it was in sacrificing those thousands of noble lives which fell upon that disastrous field, or in charging again and again upon those terrible stone walls and fortifications, after being repulsed every time with more than half their number lying on the ground. . . . But when it was proved . . . that it was morally impossible to take and retain those heights . . . which the Rebels occupied . . . whose fault was it that the attempt was made time after time, until the field was literally piled with dead and ran red with blood? We may truly say of the brave soldiers thus sacrificed,

> Theirs not to reason why,
> Theirs not to make reply,
> Theirs but to do and die.

At last a council of war was held by the generals, and it was decided that the battle should be abandoned, that the army should recross the river under the cover of darkness. This they did quietly, even partially removing the bridges before the Confederates learned of the retreat.

After the battle, the weather continued to be very cold. The troops returned to their old camps in the mud.

"The unnecessary slaughter of our men at Fredericksburg had a sad effect upon our troops, and the tone of the Northern press was truly depressing," Emma wrote.

The Union army, with 13,000 casualties, suffered one of the worst defeats of the war.

Once more, "On to Richmond" had failed.

—— 14 ——

Captured!

On January 25, 1863 General Joseph Hooker became commander of the Army of the Potomac. But Emma thought she'd like to stay with the Ninth Corps, which had now been transferred to the Western Division, the Department of the Ohio. Perhaps it was General Poe who requested that she be transferred with him. James Reid, promoted to first lieutenant, was transferred there, too.

On leaving the Army of the Potomac, Emma wrote: "The weather department is in perfect keeping with the War Department, its policy being to make as many changes as possible, and every one worse than the last. May God bless the old Army of the Potomac, and save it from annihilation."

On March 20 Emma took the train to Louisville, Kentucky. A border state, Kentucky had stayed loyal to the Union. Emma rejoined Company F of the Second Michigan Infantry, now attached to the Ninth Corps. From there she went to Lebanon to spy among local citizens.

It was evening when she came to a village and knocked on a door. A wedding party was in progress, and the house was filled with Rebel officers and guests. Captain Logan, the bridegroom, who also happened to be a recruiting officer for the Confederates, answered the door. He questioned Emma and then decided she was a true Kentuckian and all right. But why wasn't this young man in the army? Captain Logan asked. Wasn't he patriotic?

Emma turned to leave, but Captain Logan detained her. "See here, my lad," he said, "I think the best thing for you to do is to enlist, and join a company which is just forming here in the village. We are giving a bounty to all who freely enlist, and are conscripting those who refuse."

Emma said she'd like to think it over for a few days.

"But we can't wait for you to decide," the captain said. "The Yankees may be upon us at any moment, for we are not far from their lines."

Before Emma could get away, the captain placed her under guard. "You may consider yourself a soldier of the Confederacy from this hour, and subject to military discipline," he said.

"I did not despair," Emma wrote, "but trusted in Providence and my own ingenuity to escape from this dilemma."

Emma soon learned she would be in the cavalry. This encouraged her, since escape would be easier on horseback.

Her company set out at daybreak the next day. Captain Logan complimented Emma on her horsemanship. He told her she'd be grateful to him when the war was won and the South had gained its independence. "Then," he said, "you will thank me for the interest which I have taken in you and for the gentle persuasives which I made use of to stir up your patriotism and remind you of your duty to your country."

When they'd traveled for about half an hour, they met up with an advance cavalry of the Federals, and fighting broke out. Emma's horse suddenly became unmanageable and by "accident" she found herself on the Federal side of the line. Fortunately, a Federal officer recognized her, and she fell in beside him.

"That brought me face to face with my Rebel captain to whom I owed such a debt of gratitude," Emma wrote.

In battle

"Thinking this would be a good time to cancel all obligations in that direction, I discharged the contents of my pistol in his face.

"This act made me the center of attraction. Every Rebel seemed determined to have the pleasure of killing me first."

The Confederate captain was wounded badly, but not killed. The Federal infantry advanced from behind the cavalry, fought with fury, and the Rebels fled.

"I escaped without receiving a scratch," Emma wrote, "but my horse was badly cut across the neck with a saber, . . . which did not injure him materially, [but] only for a short time.

"After burying the dead, Federal and Rebel, we returned to camp with our prisoners and wounded, and I rejoiced at having once more escaped from the Confederate lines."

Did Emma actually shoot Captain Logan in the face as she claimed, or was she simply exaggerating her tale to satisfy her public and make her adventure sound more daring? Shooting someone in the face seems drastic behavior for a nurse who tenderly had cared for the sick and wounded, even a Confederate soldier on at least one occasion.

Emma was commended for her performance but was told she would not be allowed to spy in the area again, for fear of being recognized and "hung from the nearest tree."

"Not having any particular fancy for such an exalted position," Emma wrote, ". . . I turned my attention to more quiet and less dangerous duties."

Emma's quiet duty turned out to be serving as a detective

117

in Louisville, since many there were giving important information to the Confederates. Wearing ordinary clothes, she mingled among the people, making friends with Confederate sympathizers. She discovered that one of the most rabid was a merchant, so she entered his shop and asked for a job. The merchant said he would be needing someone because one of his clerks was leaving soon. But before hiring the young man before him, he wanted to know more about him, who he was, where he came from, and why he had come to Louisville.

Emma explained that she was a foreigner who wanted to see a little of the great American war and had come down South, but now being a little short of money, needed to find some employment.

"This was literally true," Emma wrote. "I was a foreigner, and very often scarce of money, and really wished him to employ me."

The merchant, satisfied with her answers, told her to report the next week. But that didn't suit Emma. She asked to start right away in order to learn her duties before the other clerk left. For that week's work, since she'd be in training, she said he could pay her whatever he chose. That pleased the merchant, and she began work at once. After being at the store for a few weeks, Emma learned the names of several spies operating within Federal lines.

Her employer often spoke about politics, but Emma said she knew little about politics in America. In fact, she said, she wasn't sure what the terms *Federal* and *Confederate* actually meant. She made mistakes in the store, and her employer kept reminding her never to call the "damned

Yankees" Confederates. He talked to her at great length, explaining the "true" state of affairs in the land. Emma paid close attention. Eventually she said she'd like to enter the Confederate service and asked if he knew how she could get across Yankee lines to enlist. The employer said he knew someone he thought could help her, a Confederate spy who often posed in Yankee camps as a Union man.

The day before her intended departure, Emma informed the Union provost marshal, suggesting that he send someone to the store the next day, when she would know all the details. She would enclose all necessary information in a package.

When she returned to the store, her employer introduced her to the man who was to conduct her through Yankee lines. The man questioned her, but Emma pretended to be "slow of speech" and referred him to her employer, who convinced him of her loyalty. "Well, I suppose if I don't like soldiering, they will let me go home again," she said, further convincing the spy of her simpleness.

The next day the provost marshal himself came into the store for his package.

At nine that night, Emma and the spy started out. The spy, anxious to impress Emma with his importance, spoke freely of his exploits and bragged about his experiences. He told her of a sutler who spied while selling supplies such as razors and watches to Union soldiers, and of another spy, a photographer, who sold pictures of Union generals at camp. Then, while they were walking along,

Union cavalrymen burst upon them and took them both prisoner. Both were searched, and documents found on Emma's companion proved he was a spy. Emma said the sutler was found and arrested, but the photographer escaped.

Her days as a detective were now over. Officers decided that it would be far too dangerous for Frank to show his face in Louisville again. Emma received more bad news. Both General Poe and James were leaving the army. Poe had been promoted to general before Fredericksburg, but the Senate had failed to confirm the promotion, and his commission in the volunteers had expired. Poe returned to his regular army status and went to Tennessee as a captain of engineers. James asked to resign because his wife was seriously ill.

Was Emma shocked on hearing that news? Had she known James was married? No one is certain. But the army accepted James's resignation and on April 22, the day he left camp, Emma deserted.

William Boston of Company H, Twenty-ninth Michigan Volunteer Infantry, was no doubt referring to Emma when he wrote in his diary:

> We are having quite a time at the expense of our brigadier postmaster. He turns out to be a girl and has deserted when her lover, Inspector Read and General Poe, resigned. She went by the name Frank Crandall and was a pretty girl. She came out with Co. F of the Second Michigan Regiment and has been with them ever since.

General John Robertson wrote in *Michigan in the War*, published in 1882:

In Company F, Second Michigan Infantry, there enlisted at Flint, Franklin Thompson (or Frank as [he was] usually called), aged 20, ascertained afterwards, and about the time he left the regiment, to have been a female, and a good-looking one at that. She succeeded in concealing her sex most admirably, serving in various campaigns and battles of the regiment as a soldier; [she was] often employed as a spy, going within the enemy's lines, sometimes absent for weeks, and is said to have furnished much valuable information. She remained with the regiment until April 1863, when it is supposed she apprehended a disclosure of her sex and deserted at Lebanon, Ky., but where she went remains a mystery.

Years later Emma claimed her illnesses caused her to leave the army. She told a reporter:

It is true that my discharge from the service did not come the way of the "red tape" line, but by a more direct route—simply that of leaving on my own account. . . . But from my standpoint I never for a moment considered myself a deserter. I simply left because I could hold out no longer, and to remain and become a helpless patient in a hospital was sure discovery, which to me was far worse than death.

No one knows exactly why Emma deserted. Perhaps the illnesses and injuries she'd suffered became too severe to ignore. Perhaps she realized then that many in the army had guessed her true sex. Or perhaps she was too upset at losing James to stay in the army without him. Besides, there were no more options open to her now. She had never been a fighting soldier and didn't wish to be one. Perhaps, too, she was tired of masquerading as a man and longed to live as a woman again.

── 15 ──

Emma Edmonds Once More

Emma, still dressed as Frank, left Lebanon, Kentucky and headed for Oberlin, Ohio. It was no accident that she chose Oberlin, probably the most liberal city in the United States. Many black Americans who had escaped slavery through the Underground Railroad found safety in Oberlin. Oberlin College was the first college in the United States to accept students regardless of color and the first college to accept women, too. This was important to Emma, who had dreams of continuing her education someday.

In Oberlin, Emma dressed as a man for a while, and perhaps rested until she felt better. Then she went to Pittsburgh, Pennsylvania, where she began wearing women's clothes. Never again did Emma pretend to be a man. She returned to Oberlin a month later and registered as Emma Edmonds at the same boardinghouse where she'd stayed before. She claimed that no one recognized her or even suspected that Emma Edmonds and Frank Thompson were one and the same person. Emma loved believing she was able to fool everyone.

She spent the following months writing memoirs that she titled: *Nurse and Spy in the Union Army: Comprising the*

A woman again

Adventures and Experiences of a Woman in Hospitals, Camps, and Battle-Fields. Emma dedicated the book to sick and wounded soldiers of the Army of the Potomac. The publishers were Hurlburt and Company, for whom Emma had once been a book salesman. They cautiously included a "Publisher's Notice"—because of then-current attitudes toward women, Hurlburt and Company felt it necessary to explain to the public that the author's disguise as a man stemmed from the purest motives (see Appendix).

Nurse and Spy became a best-seller: 175,000 copies were sold. Emma had no desire to profit from soldiers' sufferings, so she donated all her book earnings to sick and wounded soldiers. She was pleased, too, that many soldiers and widows of men who died serving their country were able to earn money by selling the book door-to-door, much as she had sold books before the war.

After completing the book, Emma felt guilty for neglecting the sick and wounded soldiers of the Union army, so she joined the Christian Commission and worked as a female nurse. In 1863 the Christian Commission had begun caring for sick and wounded soldiers of the North. Emma tended the wounded in hospitals from Harper's Ferry to Clarksburg, West Virginia, working wherever she was needed. In the fall of 1864 she went to Harper's Ferry, and it was there that she met Linus Seely, a widower and carpenter also from New Brunswick, Canada, and fell in love. It didn't take long for Linus, a quiet person, to become captivated by the dynamic Emma.

When the war ended, Emma returned to Oberlin and took some courses at the college. Linus followed and found work as a carpenter. Later that year, they both returned to Canada to visit their families.

Emma's sisters and brother were living, but her parents, Isaac and Betsy, had died. Thomas died a few years later, probably from an epileptic seizure. Some said that Isaac, in his later years, often sat by the window and looked out longingly, as if waiting for Emma's return. Perhaps he regretted his past stern behavior. But Emma never saw her father after leaving home with Miss Annie Moffitt.

For a time, Emma sold ladies' hats again, but then returned to the United States. Linus followed and they were married on April 27, 1867, at Cleveland, Ohio's fashionable Weddell House.

After the wedding, Emma wanted to change her name again. She thought an *e* at the end of Seely would make the name fancier. Emma, who had tramped through rain and mud and slept in swamps, now had a need to be fancy. Linus didn't object to the name change. He was more than willing to do whatever he could to please his bride.

The Seelye marriage was a happy one. Linus didn't mind that Emma wasn't very domestic and much preferred chopping wood to cooking. In the days before wearing long pants by women was acceptable in the United States, Emma often wore men's trousers and boots. She'd spent too many years wearing men's comfortable clothing to restrict herself to the tight-fitting women's fashions of the day.

Emma loved Linus dearly and felt loved in return, but, sadly for them, all three of their children died young. Perhaps Emma's recurring health problems made it impossible for her to bring strong and healthy children into the world. The Seelyes adopted two sons who survived.

In response to a letter from Colonel Schneider in 1900, asking about Emma, Linus wrote, "Well, her whole life was an interesting conundrum, for every week something would come up, something she could accomplish, overcome, move, or manage, that would eclipse the last."

Emma's love of traveling about never left her. The Seelyes moved often. They lived in Evanston, Illinois, for about a year before returning to Oberlin. In Oberlin, they took charge of an orphanage. Next they moved to St. Mary's Parish, Louisiana, and ran an orphanage for black children sponsored by the Freedmen's Aid Society. Emma became seriously ill during a trip to Mobile, Alabama, so they returned to Louisiana. Next they headed for California, Missouri, a small city about 150 miles from St. Louis, and lived there for two years. They spent some time in Denver, Colorado. Finally, they moved to Fort Scott, Kansas, where they stayed for twelve years. In 1883, Emma told a reporter that she and her husband "have been now for a goodly number of years very happy together."

Emma's old illnesses continued to plague her. She suffered recurring bouts of malaria. High fevers and weakness often left her bedridden for weeks. When the family suffered financial losses, friends urged her to apply for her army back pay and a soldier's pension. She had, after all, served in the United States Army for nearly two years. Finally Emma agreed, but she knew that first she'd have to prove that Sarah Emma Seelye and Frank Thompson were one and the same person.

── 16 ──

Reunion

Emma returned to Flint in 1883 and looked up her old army buddy, Damon Stewart. A series of articles by Colonel Frederick Schneider in Lansing, Michigan's *State Republican* in 1900 described Emma's visit to Flint and ensuing events.

Emma discovered that Damon owned a dry-goods store. According to the articles, Damon was sitting at a desk in his office when Emma approached. She asked if he knew the present address of Frank Thompson.

On hearing Frank's name, Damon said, his mind raced back twenty years to his old army days. He looked into the eyes of the middle-aged woman who stood before him.

"Are you his mother?" he asked.

"No, I am not his mother," Emma answered.

"His sister, perhaps?" Damon suggested.

Steps were heard approaching, so Emma took a pencil from Damon's hand and wrote quickly, "Be quiet! I am Frank Thompson!"

"What did I do next?" Damon later told his friend, A. M. G., a Flint reporter. "Sat down, I think wilted, if you please; but if I was nonplussed, the woman before me was not. She was as tranquil and self-possessed as ever my little friend Frank had been."

Damon invited Emma home to meet his wife and then sat down and wrote a note to A. M. G.: "While doing service in the Union army during the years of 1861 and 1862, I had a companion, chum, campfellow. I thought it was a man! I hope to die if it was not a woman! She's up at our house now. Come out!"

"And you never suspected the fact of her real sex?" the reporter asked Damon when they spoke.

"Never! We jested about the ridiculous little boots and called Frank 'our woman,' but he took it all in good part, and—well, Mrs. Seelye would hardly be our guest now if I remembered anything of Frank that was not straight."

After meeting Emma, the reporter wrote, "I found Mrs. S. E. Seelye, formerly Miss Sarah Edmonds, alias Frank Thompson, to be a woman between forty and fifty years of age. She has black hair and eyes, a quick, intelligent expression, and a general appearance suggesting the idea that she might have made her toilette with scrupulous care, as to neatness, but possibly without a mirror."

Emma spent the rest of her time in Flint looking up her old comrades now living in the area. She needed sworn statements from men who had known Frank and would be willing to state that Frank Thompson and Emma Seelye were the same person. William McCreery recognized Frank immediately, and others did as well. They all said they'd be willing to sign such statements.

Damon contacted other men of Company F, telling them that Frank Thompson had turned up. He broke the news that Frank Thompson was a woman named Emma Seelye and asked them to send letters to government officials on her behalf. So Emma returned to Fort Scott, Kansas, feeling her mission was accomplished.

Emma was back in Kansas when her former captain, William R. Morse, came to visit. "I was shown into a neat but plain little parlor," he reported. "In a few minutes the lady made her appearance and recognized me. I spent a very pleasant hour in talking over old times and in listening to the story of her life. . . . I do know that S. Emma Seelye is the identical Franklin Thompson."

When Judge Albert E. Cowles of Lansing, Michigan, read a newspaper account of Emma's experiences, he wrote to her and sent her his picture. Judge Cowles, formerly of the Twentieth Michigan Infantry, had served with Emma at brigade headquarters.

Emma wrote back, "Thanks, many thanks for the picture. I would gladly send you mine in return, but have none on hand, but will get some copied and send you one of 'Frank,' alias Miss E. before she was married. I think I can never be persuaded to sit for another picture.

"I have been sort of an invalid for years," she wrote, "don't go out scarcely at all, but try to do my own work, and play mother to two small boys, whose names and ages are, respectively, Frederick G. Seelye, aged eleven, and Charles G. Seelye, aged nine. . . ."

Emma's claim of poor health was supported by Thomas Barrett, M.D., of Fort Scott, Kansas, who examined Emma and found her suffering from symptoms of disease of the heart, inflammatory rheumatism, and disease of the liver, spleen, and kidney.

Colonel Schneider, past commander of the Second Michigan Volunteer Infantry and now post commander in Flint, invited Emma to the next army reunion. Emma answered in a letter to Judge Cowles:

> Your great kindness and delicate consideration entitles you to my warmest gratitude and thanks. I cannot express to you how much I feel moved by the invitation to be present at the reunion of the noble survivors of the Second Michigan Infantry—every one of whom I love as if they were my own brothers . . . but unfortunately I am quite out of health, much more so than usual, for I am writing this in bed, not being able to sit up.
>
> Thanks to William Shakespeare for his card; he and I used to be "boys together" in the hospital. I remember him well. . . .
>
> P.S. Please say to Colonel Schneider that I ask, as a favor of all my friends of the Second, that they, each and every one of them, send me a picture of himself in uniform; and will you be kind enough to send me that picture of yourself as you are now, which you promised me.

The judge sent her a group picture taken of the survivors of the Second Michigan Infantry as they posed in front of the state capitol at their reunion, October 11, 1883. Emma wrote Cowles that she was so delighted with the picture that she wept.

Emma's comrades invited her to their next army reunion. This time Emma accepted, and men who had known Frank as their postmaster gathered around and exchanged memories with the plump, middle-aged matron. A special program was planned. General Poe, William Shakespeare, and Captain Morse all gave speeches; a local glee club sang; Gardner's Flint Band provided more music; and a recitation by Mrs. O. F. Lockhead was given. But everyone agreed that the highlight of the afternoon occurred when Emma herself addressed the group:

"My dear comrades, my heart is so full I cannot say what I would to you. Tears are in my eyes, but I shall never, never forget your love and kindness to Frank Thompson. All that I can say is that I am deeply grateful, and may God bless you."

After the reunion, the only army reunion Emma ever attended, she kept in touch with some of her comrades, Richard Halsted and Robert Bostwick in particular. But she was upset to learn that gossip about her had begun circulating. Apparently not everyone believed her claim that she had left the army because she was sick and feared discovery. The reunion, too, might have brought back bittersweet memories of loves not entirely forgotten, even after all those years.

Emma had other problems besides gossip facing her now. Before she could receive her pension, she still would have to prove that Emma Seelye and Frank Thompson were the same person, and the charge of desertion would have to be removed from her record.

Men who had known Emma in the army and who now held high positions of honor and trust sent individual affidavits to Congress identifying Emma with Frank Thompson. Bill H.R. 5335 was introduced to clear her name.

Former governor E. B. Winans, a member of Congress

from the Michigan's Sixth District, reported on bill H.R. 5335, stating:

> Though by the rules of war a deserter, yet . . . her course and conduct after the war shows the same zeal in the service of her country in her proper character as activated her when she first dedicated herself to the cause which she felt to be the highest and noblest that can actuate man or woman.

Included in that report was a letter sent by officers and privates of the late Second Regiment of Michigan Infantry:

> In view of her many ministrations of tenderness and mercy, thousands of soldiers who were the recipients of her timely attention and nursing must remember her with the most filial regard.
>
> She is now the same true, loyal woman that she was in those eventful, stormy days of 1861 to 1865, when the country was passing [through] the agonizing throes of civil war. . . .

The report went on to discuss Emma's poor health and resulting great need.

The case dragged on, in spite of the efforts of Congressman Byron M. Cutcheon of the Michigan's Ninth District and former colonel of the Twentieth Michigan Infantry. Many congressmen seemed reluctant to grant a woman a Civil War army pension. Perhaps some congressmen found it hard to believe that a woman had actually served in the United States Army during the Civil War. At last a report filed by Congressman Cutcheon that included a letter from former General Poe quieted their objections. But not all of General Poe's statements were complimentary to Emma:

As a soldier, "Frank Thompson" was effeminate-looking, and for that reason was detailed as mail carrier, to avoid taking an efficient soldier from the ranks. As a woman she is masculine-looking. But a single glance at her in her proper character caused me to wonder how I could ever have mistaken her for a man, and I readily recall many things that could have betrayed her, except that no one thought of finding a woman in soldier's dress. I don't think I could be deceived that way again, even if, as was the case, the whole regiment was in ignorance regarding the matter.

As a soldier, "Frank Thompson" did her duty to the best of her ability as long as she remained with the regiment.

Please let me know if an affidavit is wanted from me and others, or if this is sufficient. There is plenty of testimony in this case. . . .

Congressman Cutcheon stated in one report, "As this remarkable case can hardly be objected to on the ground that it is likely to set a precedent, the committee recommends that the bill do pass."

Finally, on July 7, 1886, President Grover Cleveland signed a bill that removed the charge of desertion from Franklin Thompson's record, allowing Emma to receive her pension. Emma wrote to Congressman Cutcheon thanking him for his efforts, and he answered:

> . . . for though you don't remember Major Cutcheon of the Twentieth, I remember Frank Thompson as an orderly, very well. I saw you almost every day at Fredericksburg. Now make your application to William A. Day, second auditor, for your back pay and any balance of bounty that may be due, send to me, and I will see that it is attended to.

Emma wasn't quite sure what she wanted to do with the money. She thought of building a home for soldiers who had fought for the Union but were now living in county poorhouses. Since her pension and back pay turned out to be less than expected, that plan never materialized.

Emma and Linus were living in La Porte, Texas, when Emma, as a veteran of the Grand Army of the Republic, asked to join the George B. McClellan Post No. 9, Department of Texas. Since her discharge papers were in good order then, her membership was accepted and she became the only female member.

Emma's health continued to fail and she died September 5, 1898, in La Porte. But after the funeral, her former comrades thought she should have been buried in a military cemetery. So, on Memorial Day in 1901, her body was moved to a Grand Army of the Republic plot in Washington Cemetery in Houston, Texas. She is believed to be the only woman buried there. A limestone marker reads:

EMMA E. SEELYE, ARMY NURSE

Appendix

PUBLISHER'S NOTICE

[Reprinted from 1865 edition of *Nurse and Spy*]

No apology is necessary for adding one more to the numerous "War Books" which already fill a large space in American Literature; for, to the general reader, nothing connected with the Rebellion can be more interesting than the personal experiences of those who have been intimately associated with the different phases of military life, in Camp, Field, and Hospital.

The "Nurse and Spy" is simply a record of events which have transpired in the experience and under the observation of one who has been on the field and participated in numerous battles—among which are the first and second Bull Run, Williamsburg, Fair Oaks, the seven days in front of Richmond, Antietam, and Fredericksburg—serving in the capacity of "Spy" and as "Field Nurse" for over two years.

While in the "Secret Service" as a "Spy," which is one of the most hazardous positions in the army—she penetrated the enemy's lines, in various disguises, no less than eleven times; always with complete success and without detection.

Her efficient labors in the different Hospitals as well as her arduous duties as "Field Nurse," embrace many thrilling and touching incidents, which are here most graphically described.

Should any of her readers object to some of her disguises, it may be sufficient to remind them it was from the purest motives and most praiseworthy patriotism, that she laid aside, for a time, her own costume, and assumed that of the opposite sex, enduring hardships, suffering untold privations, and hazarding her life for her adopted country, in its trying hour of need.

In the opinion of many, it is the privilege of woman to minister to the sick and soothe the sorrowing—and in the present crisis of our country's history, to aid our brothers to the extent of her capacity—and whether duty leads her to the couch of luxury, the abode of poverty, the crowded hospital, or the terrible battlefield—it makes but little difference what costume she assumes while in the discharge of her duties. Perhaps she should have the privilege of choosing herself whatever may be the surest protection from insult and inconvenience in her blessed, self-sacrificing work.

The moral character of the work—being true to virtue, patriotism, and philanthropy—together with the fine embellishments and neat mechanical execution—will, we trust, render it an interesting and welcome visitor at every fireside.

Sources

Bailey, Ronald H. *Forward to Richmond: McClellan's Peninsula Campaign.* Alexandria, VA: Time-Life Books, 1983.

—— *The Bloodiest Day: The Battle of Antietam.* Alexandria, VA: Time-Life Books, 1983.

Catton, Bruce. *Terrible Swift Sword, Vol. II.* New York: Doubleday, 1963.

—— *The Civil War.* New York: American Heritage Press, 1971.

—— *Reflections on the Civil War.* Edited by John Leekley. New York: Berkley Books, 1982.

—— *American Heritage Picture History of the Civil War.* New York, 1960.

Dannett, Sylvia G. L. *She Rode with the Generals.* New York: Thomas Nelson & Sons, 1960.

Davis, William C. *First Blood: Ft. Sumter to Bull Run.* Alexandria, VA: Time-Life Books, 1983.

Edmonds, S. Emma E. *Nurse and Spy in the Union Army: Comprising the Adventures and Experiences of a Woman in Hospitals, Camps and Battle-Fields.* Hartford, CT: W. S. Williams & Co., 1865.

Faust, Patricia L., ed. *Historical Times Illustrated Encyclopedia of the Civil War.* New York: Harper & Row, 1986.

Hanson, Harry. *The Civil War.* New York: Duell, Sloan & Pearce, 1961.

Lee Takes Command: From Seven Days to Bull Run. Alexandria, VA: Time-Life Books, 1983.

Long, E. B., with Barbara Long. *Civil War Day by Day: An Almanac 1861–1865.* New York: Doubleday, 1971.

McPherson, James M. *Battle Cry of Freedom: The Civil War Era.* New York: Oxford University Press, 1988.

Nevins, Allan. *The War for the Union, Vol. II: War Becomes Revolution.* New York: Charles Scribner's Sons, 1960.

Smith, Page. *Trial by Fire.* New York: McGraw-Hill, 1982.

Index

143

Varney, James, 32
Varney, James A., 32

Williamsburg, battle of, 67
Will Jones Resolve, 50

Winans, E. B., 132–33
Wolverine Citizen, 90

Yorktown, 51–52, 63–64, 84

921
EDM

Stevens, Bryna

Frank Thompson

$13.95

10423

DATE			
FE 9 '95 461			
18 00			
19